ACROSS
THE BRIDGE

ACROSS
THE BRIDGE

J.W. BLACKBURN

Contents

There are stories many that's to be told
Some stories last a lifetime
Others last just through the day
Stories handed down for thousands of years
Those stories, are they true or false?
The stories and poems that are in this book
Some are true, most are not
If just one of these poems or stories changes someone
For the better, then it was worth it . . . What I have written down
comes from within

I dedicate this book to Eugene H. Wagner, veteran of the US Navy,
World War II.
For after each poem or story I read to him, he would nod his head or
tell me to change this to that. Gene is my friend, and we are brothers
in Christ.

And also to my sister Shirley Dempsey and her husband Lawrence
for their support through bad times and good times.

And above all, to my God, for without him, there is nothing.

PART ONE

God and His Wonders

IN THE BEGINNING

In the beginning there was nothing
In the beginning there was the word
And the word it's called salvation
Salvation through Christ our Lord

In the beginning there was nothing
In the beginning God created the world
And in that world God did create them
Male and female to serve Yahweh, God our Lord

In the beginning God did create them
Wonders like never been seen before
And gave us the dominion to oversee them
Beast of the earth, fish of the sea
The birds he also made them to soar
Throughout the heavens above
God created them just for you and me

As time passed throughout the ages
Bad things happening throughout the world
We abuse them, and did so too our brothern
So he sent us his only beloved
That whosoever believeth in him shall
Not die, but live eternal through
Jesus Christ our Lord.

In the beginning there was nothing
And the beginning, yes, there was the word
And yes, the word it's still called
Salvation
Salvation through Jesus, the Christ
Our Lord

THE SPIRIT OF GOD

I am a traveler. I travel near and far. I have traveled the world over. Yes, I am the spirit of God.

I have traveled the earth and, yes, the universe even before the beginning of time. I know all there is to know. I am the spirit of God. He created life as you see it, he created life long time past, and he created those giants that you now dig up. I know—for I am the spirit of God.

God in the beginning created the garden called Eden and all that was within. He then created male and female; he named the male Adam, the female Eve. He walked and talked with them. I know, for I am the spirit of God. From Adam and Eve down to Noah and his ark, to Abraham, Isaac, and Jacob even to Lot—I knew them all, and to them they did know me. I am the spirit of God. I went with Moses and his people. I led them by day and by night, by day a cloud, by night a pillar of fire, for I am the spirit of God. Moses went up to the mountains, and there he saw a burning bush and fell to his knees, and God spoke to him. I know, for I was there. I am the spirit of God. Down through the ages from Moses and the law, to Joshua and the kings and to his servant David who united the tribes, to Solomon and the temple to Babylon and then Rome, I was there and saw it all, for I am the spirit of God.

Then God sent his servant Gabriel to a young woman and told her what was to come. She was to conceive and bear a son, God's son, for I know I am that son. I am the Son of God.

I'm with you today as I was at the beginning of time. I will be with you all, if only you believe and be with you forevermore, till the end of time and beyond.

For I am he, Jesus the Jewish Messiah. I am the Son of God.

GOD AND THE HEAVENS

As I stand and look out into the heavens, seeing bright lights from a far distance away, I wonder why they were created, all those stars, planets, billions of light-years away. Then I stop and look around me then remember some who say we are all atoms. Everything, even you and me, so they say. Then something lights up inside me, something so bright and yet so warm. The light, it comes and surrounds me. My inner being is full of joy. I ask myself what is happening, then something from the light, like a thought, a dream, a vision says I am he that created you, all that you see and all you cannot see. I am the past, present, and future, the beginning and the ending. I created the heavens and the earth and all that there is. So look out into the heavens; there are wonders to behold. Yes, you ask why so many are there. Stars, planets, and yes, even black holes. The thought he tells me I am that I am, there is no other.

It took me six days to do what I wanted to do, but it could have taken me only a wink of an eye. For me there is no time as you see it. I see into the future. I see man and what he is capable to be. I know today they will say it took five billion years to create all from the so-called big bang theory. I knew then what man would be thinking today. I made it so, like babble confused. If there are others out there in this vast darkness of space, would they rather be like you or like other form of life? And if so, remember I created them too. For

15

there is nothing I did not create. I created male and female on the sixth day. I say sixth day on your time not mine and gave them the world—to go out and be fruitful and multiply and plenish the earth. I gave them and you all that are in it, on, and above the earth for your kindred to tend and be caretakers of all living and nonliving things and what you call our mother earth. There is no mother earth, only me and the word.

I see abuse from all, and yet to some, I see that they are trying to help. As I created you from the beginning, it follows you all. This greed, yes, it follows you and puts evil in your heart where the word should be. Yes, this greed, also called envy, lust, hate, jealousy, lies and more. It must pass, and one day the word and I, and I alone, know the day and hour. It will pass this world, this universe. Then a new heaven and a new earth shall I create. Away with the old; I will remember it no more. For then you and your kind will turn to me, your Creator and God, with the words "my son," then I may let you see all. And then the light blessed me, and I accepted the words "his son." Now as I look out into the heavens, I see anew, for the Creator and I call him God. He is here and out there, and he is still creating as I smile and pray and thank him for everything. Why? you ask. Because he created everything that was and is and is to come, so look out in the heavens. See all the galaxies, billions of them and trillions of stars and planets in each. And I smile, and still you ask why. Because he created me, that's why.

GOD'S UNIVERSE

As I stand on top of a mountain at night far away from the city lights, and as I look out into the heavens, I see all those stars that shine our way. I wonder, are we alone in this darkness that we call the universe? Then my mind wonders back in time. Were the stars just put there for mankind? If so, why are there so many, billions of them? Most we don't see, but are they out there just for you and me? The sun gives us light and warmth by day, the moon and stars at night to guide us on our way. So man has done wonders since his short time here on earth. Man on the moon, crafts to Mars, Jupiter, and far beyond in deep space. The Hubble telescope that sees so far, sending back pictures of galaxies so fast that they blow our mind, billions of them and trillions of stars and planets in each. Are we alone in the universe, or are there others out there thinking the same as we?

God created the universe and all that's within. God created us, why not them? God gave us a mind to think and to reason. Yes, we have great potential. As the human race, we will one day—if we're still around—explore the heavens and leave our home and find a new one many light-years away. But for now, as I look down and see, we must overcome our problems here on earth before going off to explore new worlds. Or were we meant to stay here, on earth, our home? Or will he allow us to explore his vast universe? Only time will tell and only by his request. It's God's creation, and only he knows best.

THE BIBLE

Have you ever wondered what it would be like to live in a world of peace and love? No more fighting, no more wars, no more hate, a world where neighbors know their neighbors and there are no locks on the doors. Have you, just for a second or more, then sat back and smiled and see things happening even if they were only in your dream? And you look around you; you see a book. It's covered in dust and no one has touch it or read it, and you ask yourself how did it get here, who brought it in, for it's not yours. You have never read it. It's just a bunch of stories that man has written down. You have heard them from the time when you were a kid and seen movies of them that Hollywood made. Now you're staring at the book that does not belong in your home, for you believe, like a lot of scientists believe, that we started in the sea; and over millions of years, we evolved to what we are if you look in a mirror. And when we get old like everything does, we die, and that's the end. There's no afterlife, no being born again. So your family, if you have one, will bury you and get on with their lives. Now you're staring at the book, and it draws you to it. And you can't resist. So you pick it up and look at the age-old leather that's worn and beaten down. The gold lettering is fading but still stands out; it still can be seen. So you dust it off and begin to read. The pages are all worn and brown. As you turn to the first book and begin to read in the beginning and you read even more, and as you read, a spark glows inside and it burns bright. It opens up your eyes, and as you read, you fight back the tears.

You read of Adam and Eve, Noah and the ark of Abraham, Isaac and Jacob, to Moses to David and more reading of wars on top of wars, conquer or be conquered. To their laws and beliefs. Yes, even how to bathe and bury the dead. As you read, a new page appears. It's called the New Testament. And it begins, "In the beginning was the word, and the word was with God, and the word was God." As you read more, tears fall down your cheek. As you read the words, they change: from a seed in a womb, to birth, to a man and he, according to the word, was sent here to redeem the world that whosoever believes in him will live with him forevermore. As you read, your mind and heart went back to that day, that same very spot, and you saw what you had read. They took him out and nailed him to a cross with two others. One on each side, they were thieves. One said, "Save yourself." But the other saw into his eyes and said, "Rabbi, remember me," and Jesus said, "For that is his name today, you shall be with me in paradise." Then they took him down and laid him in a tomb close by.

They put guards to guard his tomb, and you wondered why, for they nailed him to a cross. Now he's dead. Then your mind and soul floated past to the third day. As the sun came up and as you looked and there were no guards, the stone block had been rolled away. You looked inside, and there was no body to be seen. Then you saw the man standing all anew, talking to some women that he once knew. As you watched, you started to understand those words of Jeremiah; they came back to you. For he is the redeemer, yes, he is the word. You read page after page; then the last book unfolded, and it took your breath away of things that were to come. On that day, and only God knows, the great book will be open, and the names shall be read. You cry and pray to God that your name is written in the book. Then that glow that came from within lifted your soul to the one that was nailed to the cross so long ago. Then you opened your eyes and heart, and you looked down at the book. The cover that was worn and weathered again became new. The pages inside, instead of brown, were crisp and clean like new. Then someone inside deep down said to be at peace and with good cheer goes out and spreads the good news that Jesus Christ is here.

THE STAR

As I lay in bed, I dreamed of that night, that holy night when the stars were out so very bright.

As I dreamed, I saw there was one bright star, brighter than all the other stars combined, moving across the heavens by an invisible hand. As I got closer, I saw the star, and it settled over a manger in a small town called Bethlehem.

Then I heard, with great delight, all the angels in heaven singing, "Glory to God in the highest, for unto this night a child is born, and he shall rule his kingdom, this earth, forevermore."

As the angels in heaven sang, one came down and told the shepherds in the field, "Rejoice, for whom you have waited for has now been born." When they heard this, they were afraid, but they rejoiced at what they were told and went to see. And they saw and they smiled as they looked at the child. They bowed their heads and prayed to God the most high.

Then I saw out of the east, three did come. Seeing a star, it guided them to where the child was born. They presented him with gifts, prayed, then departed another way.

Oh, this star so mighty and bright, you were given the honor above all those stars in heaven that night.

You with the movement of the Father's hands, you moved across the heavens, and only a few would see, to settle above a manger in Bethlehem.

As I dreamed, I smiled and prayed with great delight, wondering where's that star that shined so bright that night. Then from deep, deep down inside, one was speaking to me but not out loud, saying, "The star you see in your dream is the same star the wise men and shepherds saw."

For that star was the Father's hand, so remember your dream; remember that night. God gave the world—yes, the whole world—his only son that night. And I rejoiced and prayed to God the most high, knowing that one day, and only the Father knows when, I will see his son ruling his people with pure love and sitting on the throne of David high on the mount in the holiest city of them all—Jerusalem.

THE MAN

In a time, it does not matter where or when, man will walk the earth again and again. From the beginning until now, man has fought wars over that secret place, that holy place that's called Jerusalem, that place where Abraham and Sarah and the prophets are buried in the ground and near a place where a child was born and after which Rachel mourned, a place of beauty where miracles and wonders were performed. A place where the most high is to make his home and the child grew to be a man. He took twelve from their place of work and said, "Follow me. I'll make you fishers of men." He took them near and far and preached the Word of God in everybody's ear and put into their hearts and minds lots of things that they had left far behind. For they had given up, with no hope, for the Romans conquered them without remorse and brought in their gods in this holy place. Then evil and corruption followed as it had always done and went into every place, even the most holy of places.

And this evil one, he smiled as it was being done. Then another man came. He preached the Word of God and was baptizing in God's name. He told the people there about one "that would come after me but is before me and before you." And that "he will change the world, make it a better place." The man came, was baptized, and after that, the man departed and went up into the mountains—or the wilderness, it was called—for forty days and nights. He did not eat or drink but fasted and prayed. Then someone came, someone he knew; from the beginning of time, he knew. This deceiver of man, even in the garden he knew. This Satan—that was his name—laughed and mocked the man and said many things, but the man turned away.

Finally, after a time, Satan said, "Look what I've got." And he showed the man all the kingdoms of the earth, then and now, even beyond. "I'll give all this to you. Do with it as you please, but only worship me." The man, with his hand pointed at Satan, said, "Get behind me. I worship thy God, and only him I serve." And then Satan left the man, and angels came and tended to him. Afterward, he took the twelve. They preached the good news, but the one that could change him not, he put all his evilness into man's heart, one then betrayed him. The priest then took this man away. Took him before Pilate, they and the Romans, they crucified him. This was not the end as some would have thought because on the third day he arose from death, and death went away.

Satan saw and said to himself, "I'll get even with you by other means." Then he went away. Some of his own who saw the man dead but now alive went and spread the word. Some did not recognize him, for he himself had changed in some way. He showed them proof who he was. They knelt before him and prayed. Then on that mountain that stood so high, he ascended up in the sky. The twelve and others did his work and spread the gospel far and about even to Rome itself. Others went different ways and spread the news, but the seed of the evil one spread more than ever, to Rome and in the hearts of the Romans, to Nero himself. He sent these followers of the man who died on the cross to their deaths and laughed at them as they prayed, and thousands upon thousands lost their lives that way. Then in time one saw the light, a bright cross he saw. So he freed them, these Christians they were called, and became one himself after all. Then it happened like wildfire on the open plains.

This Christian faith, it grew and grew. Until today, millions upon millions pray to God in this man's name. But Satan is still here, out here in our midst, preying on men's hearts as he looks from afar and up close, knowing it's only a matter of time before his final days are due. So as of today, same as then, men are fighting over and for that holy place. It's a state with enemies all around. Who is to help them, this state with enemies all around? So read the book, that holy book, read the last one that was written by a man called John. The words on those pages put fear and love in everyone's heart.

Bad times will come. We must keep the faith in God dear to our heart, and they will fight for that place, rich and poor, from all walks of life being deceived with that mark. They will fight but not from their hearts. They see the heavens open up, and he that cometh on a white horse, a warrior with a two-edged sword from his mouth. He and his angels, tens of thousands to behold, the men upon the ground see the man wearing a crown. Fear breaks out among the ranks. They try to flee, but they can't, for the mark they obtained kept them firm on the ground. When the battle starts, it will be finished in a flash, for the man that I speak of has been here before the beginning of time itself. He walked with God his Father in the garden, and he will walk with you. You only have to believe and call upon his name.

His name is Jesus. He is the Jewish Messiah. He is truth, and he is just. He is the Son of God.

PARADISE

As I prepare myself for bed, I thank my God I'm alive not dead. If I were dead, that would be all right, for I know I would be with him in that place that's called paradise. Some say it's on the other side, that place that is so beautiful it's beyond belief. A place where you're given new bodies and are in perfect health. You live with your Creator for eternity. That's the place where I want to be, but yet we live here on this plane of existence. We want to stay here as long as we can. Yes, we're humans. As humans, we all have excuses. From "let me get my house in order," "I want to see my children grow up," "I want to see my grandkids before I die," to "I want my grandkids get to know me." Yes, we all have excuses. Remember that we are born, we grow up, and then we die. I believe we all have a date, some call, with Mr. Death or the angel of death.

When that time comes, no matter where we're at, what we're doing, whether we are in perfect or very bad health, we're going to die. For when that time comes, be prepared, not material-wise but spiritual-wise. That's what the Lord says. And truly ask for forgiveness, for he forgives in a twinkle of an eye. Can you imagine living with God and his Son in paradise, where there will be no tears, no wars, no hardships, no death? Those three words that we hear all the time, they will not exist. Those three words—greed, envy, and hate. Can you imagine a place so beautiful? Yes, it's hard to believe that after looking at our own earth and what we, the human race, have done to it and to each other. Ever since Adam and Eve, wars upon wars, father against son. Daughter against mother, our life here's a mess; it goes on and on. It will continue as long as the evil one is still around.

Then one day, as the Good Book says, all things must come to an end. There will be one last battle. All the world will join in on one side or the other; God in all his mercy will give you a choice. It's simple. Accept him and live forever, or the other, if you choose the other, surely you will die. As for me, I want to live forever in that place called paradise, for I don't want to die. I know my body will give out someday, that one day my body will die, and in time it will turn back to dust. But my soul, my spirit belongs to God, and he wants it back. He doesn't demand it. It's up to us. When we accept God and truly believe, then we as the spirit will live forever. If we don't accept him, then yes, we will surely die, and God will remember us no more. But to live forever with God in his home, now that's where I want to be. So read the Good Book. Read it all the way through. Then in time you will understand. When that time comes you will know; then you will know that the Bible is the living Word of God. Because God will be talking back to you.

THE CREATION

In a time long before the creation of man.

God created the heavens and the earth with a thought or maybe the wave of his hand.

And with that thought wonders he did create, galaxies after galaxies with billions of stars in each.

From all those galaxies he created a special one that stretches across the universe as far as the human eye can see.

In that galaxy at the edge of one of its arms, he combined many atoms and formed what he called the earth and other bodies including a yellow ball of light he called the sun.

Then he put the earth and the other bodies all in a special place, made them spin around this yellow ball of light to create what we call our solar system.

Then he looked and smiled at the earth, saying, "I will make you far greater than all the rest combined." So he looked at the earth and changed it many, many times.

And during those times, the earth it did change. After eons and eons and eons of time, again he looked at the earth. "Now I will change you again, maybe for the last time."

And with his thought, he brought life to this barren place. Even from high in the heavens, one could see the changes he had made. From the heavens it was a beautiful blue orb down close to the ground. It was a rainbow of color, with mountains so high they did touch the sky. He separated what he called land, made rivers, lakes, oceans, and seas. He put living things in those waters, told them these waters is your home for you to roam and swim free.

"The dry land is for other species I will create, including one that will have dominion over all." He then created man (the human race).

Saying "I will create man in my image," so in his image he created man. Also from man he created woman, told them be fruitful and multiply and plenish the earth.

Now after eons, and eons of time, this man and woman—their name Adam and Eve—did what their Creator asked for. Through their descendants. They covered the earth. Out of their seed were born different races. Yes, they moved to different places and covered the entire earth.

Now these humans, they live in a time that they describe as the space age. They're smart, and they have built ships that reached out past their home, this earth. Yes, they have even set foot on the moon.

Built machines, put them in space, and now they look through what they call the telescope and see these galaxies that's on the other side of the universe, so beautiful it's beyond belief.

They see galaxies larger than our own with billions of more stars and planets in each.

They ask themselves, "Are we alone in this vast universe, or are there others out there thinking the same as we? Are we alone, us, the human race?" Only time will tell.

Only the Creator knows. Maybe in time, he may let us in on his agenda, or maybe not. He gave us over time. Prophets and seers, hints of what was to come through such men as Ezekiel, Daniel, and yes, even John then in that time, for he and only he knows the day and hour as he looked at the earth in the beginning, saying, "Yes, I have decided I will do this one last time. On that day and hour, I will create a new heaven and a new earth, for it will be the last time."

HEAVEN

There is a place, where it's at, I do not know, a place more perfect than Eden, and that's where I want to go. From what I've read, people go there and don't want to come back, for it must be something like no other, a place we dream of in our dreams. Is that place heaven? For when people die, they have never come back to complain. We have heard people say they died and saw a bright light, and yes, they wanted to stay, but something would tell them from deep inside, "You must go back, it is not your time." And they return totally different, with a story they are eager to tell. They say they died and went to the depths of hell with things indescribable clawing at them from all sides, trying to pull them deeper still. They cried and prayed, seeing a bright light above. The more they pray, the brighter and bigger it got. And those things, those demons, they flee and try to hide and run away.

Then they were engulfed with that bright and wonderful light. They saw a bridge, and on the other side, they saw something so beautiful that they couldn't even describe. They wanted to cross and were told they could not. For it was not their time. Then they were staring down at themselves, doctors and nurses standing around shaking their heads and saying "We have done all we can" as they placed the sheet over his face. They heard a grasp and then a breath. They pronounced him dead; they signed the papers. "It's just a reaction," they said as they started to take him away. Then he opened his eyes and began to speak, telling them what had happened, even watching them from above. These stories we have heard time and time again. Is it true? Some have told the doctors what they have said even after they signed the papers stating that they were dead. For most of us, yes, we believe there is a heaven for you and me and that when it's our time, we will leave and cross that bridge and not look back.

Will that time be at the moment of our death, or will it be on that last day when he will judge us all? The story of heaven and hell, it's been around before the beginning of time. We don't know the full story and probably never will. It's a battle, and it's going on still. Both want our soul and neither are giving up. So when they say they died and saw the light and returned, just maybe it was for our benefit that they came back to tell their story, what they saw, the good and the bad. For our soul is a part of God, and he wants us to return to the fold. He sent his Son to die for us. And he ascended back to him, just like someday will happen to you and to me. When someone says they died and saw the light and doctors say they were dead and they do have the proof, thank God they are telling the story. To some it will be hard to believe; to others it's hope that there is a hereafter. And that place that's called heaven is here—for it's in my heart.

GOD

God, he has been around before the beginning of time and will be around still after we all have been gone. Who is this? Someone that's older than the seas, older than the universe itself. Who is this, this God? In the beginning it's said God created the heaven and the earth. He also said before the beginning, there was nothing. I have never seen nothing, so how can I describe what I can't see? So where does God come from, and where does he call home? I don't know, for he has never said. He just mentions heaven—is that where he lays his head? I don't know. As for me, it's no big concern. I read his word; I believe in his saying. I believe in his love.

We have all wondered from time to time about where God came from and where he has been around all this time—I believe he calls heaven his home. It must be different than here on earth, for it's been around a mighty long time, and the Good Book mentions a war in heaven, someone trying to overthrow God and take over the throne. For I believe there can be only one God, for there can be no other. For if there were other gods, they would be fighting each other to see who would come out on top and who would sit on the throne. And this war in heaven, well, the aggressor, yes, he lost.

So this God, we call him by many names, and I guess he doesn't mind as long as you believe there is but one God, and that God is him—the God of Abraham, Isaac, and Jacob. To Moses he said, "I am that I am," and he said, "I will send my Son, and my Son will judge you all on that day. For a part of me is inside each and every one. And I don't want them to go astray." For there's a mystery to God, and we will never know. For in the end, it does not matter as long as we're with him.

WAR IN HEAVEN

As I sat, I wondered about many things, things that were happening now and things that happened back then. I read in the Bible before the beginning of time that there was a war in heaven, and it blew my mind—I read it in the book; it happened before mankind. How could such a thing happen, and why did it happen in God's own backyard? Yes, Satan and his followers tried to overthrow God's domain, so he fought Michael and his angels—and Michael gained the upper hand. And God cast Satan and his followers in the earth instead of destroying them. So as I sat, I wondered.

The same is happening to us today. Revenge, that's what it must be—Satan is taking his revenge out on mankind to get back to God and to gain the upper hand. Yes, he'll try to take over heaven once again. He will use us to his own advantage; he's good at this. For he is the manipulator. He is the best. He'll use us to wage war with one another. Kill or be killed, it does not matter to him. For he tried it with the anointed one in the wilderness way back then, so he uses mankind to justify his own means, and he has won many a battle, but the big one will soon begin. So he will use man and take as many with him. As he can, for he knows when that last battle occurs, and it's at Armageddon.

That he and all his followers will be cast in a lake of fire and brimstone with angels at the rim, in which he knows there is no escape.

And God with all his angels and those that believe in him on earth will live together forever in a new heaven and a new earth.

EASTER

As I lay me down to sleep, I pray to God for my soul he should keep as I drifted off in that slumber between midnight and dawn. I awake and find myself in a strange but beautiful place, and yet I know where I am. As I look around, the landscape is there, but everything else has changed. No tall buildings high in the sky, no paved roads to let the cars go by. I know this is only a dream, but the taste, the smell, and the touch is making it so real. So I close my eyes, and yet I still see. I'm standing high on the temple mount and watching all the people as they go by. And I'm wondering what I am doing here and what this is all about, and a voice comes to me and says, "Come. I'll show you what it's all about." And my spirit goes from the present back into the past. And I see and know this place, this Jerusalem, in a totally different light. I see the temple as it stood two thousand years ago. And priests going about their daily chores, Roman soldiers standing guard on every corner, making sure no one breaks their law. And then I knew this was Passover week. All Jews from far and wide descend on Jerusalem and the city bulges from all sides, for there has been unrest for many a year from Roman occupation—a thorn in the peoples' side. Taxes on taxes, it's hard to keep a family alive, and all roads that lead to Jerusalem are lined with people on crosses—all dead.

The Romans have a motto, and it's harsh and it's for all—obey our rules, or this will happen to you all. Then the voice says, "Now you see, but do you want to see it all?" As I looked all around, I wanted to see the truth. I wanted to see it all. And then before my eyes, faster than what you see on TV, the truth starts to unfold right before my very eyes. I see a man with others by his side, sitting at a table in an upper room above an inn. The ceders has just begun, like every year since Moses led the Hebrews from Egypt to the promised land. Then one man leaves—the others stay behind. Then like the speed of light, I'm in a garden. And one is praying and blood in the form of sweat runs down his face while the others slept the night away. And then noises are heard, torches are being carried by soldiers, and the man that left the room came up to the man called Jesus, kissed him, then the soldiers led this Jesus away.

As they led him away, I said no more, for I knew what was in store. But the voice said, "You wanted the truth, now you shall see." In a blink of an eye, he, Jesus, was before Pilate; and as the Pharisees looked on, I could see it all, for I had a front-row seat. Pilate knew this man and that all the evidence pointed that this man had done no wrong, but to keep the peace, for he knew what had to be done, he condemned this man. This Jesus, he condemned him to death. I did not want to go, but the spirit took me, and there I saw them beating him until he could hardly crawl. They put a crossbeam on his shoulders and made him carry it like they did to all, to a place of his execution—Golgotha, a place of the skull. They stripped him and nailed his hands and feet and lifted him up, so everyone could see. And I in my spirit, I knelt and began to pray. How many times have you heard people say they wished they were there? Yes, there to see it all.

I wanted to turn back. I wanted to awake; then I saw two men, both on a cross, on either side of him. One said, "Get down, save yourself and us all." But the other looked at Jesus and said, "Rabbi, remember me when you get to heaven." And with a smile, Jesus said, "Today you shall be with me in paradise." Then he bowed his head and he died. Then the heavens opened up, and I heard the angels cry. The earth stood still, the sun turned black, and earthquakes shook the ground. And a centurion standing guard said, "Truly, this was the Son of God." As I was crying, tears running down my face, I saw them take him down and put him in a tomb, not too far away. Then the spirit carried me to the first day of the week. I'm in front of the tomb, and the stone had been rolled away. Two women that he knew came as is their tradition to wash and cleansed the body of the man they once knew.

When they entered the tomb, he was no longer there. An angel appeared and told them to go and spread the good news that Jesus had risen and was alive. And as I closed my eyes and began to pray, the angel told me to go outside and see who's there. And lo and behold, the man that had been dead was standing before my very eyes, radiant and aglow and dressed in the whitest of white and a golden girdle wrapped around his waist. He was smiling with those beautiful and penetrating eyes.

I fell to my knees and praised God the most high, and then a voice from heaven said, "This is my son, and I am very well pleased." Then his hand touched my face, and I was filled with his love and his grace. "What you have seen in your dream, John, is the truth. Let no man take it away. Now go back to your time and spread the good news that I will come again and I will judge, yes, judge you all. When I return, I will create a new heaven and a new earth. I will sit on my Father's throne and rule you all with pure love—not hate. Until that time, you must keep the faith." Then I opened my eyes and was wide awake. I was on my knees and out of bed, and my body was soaked in sweat, for this dream was beyond belief. Then I looked closer. My shirt was soaked in sweat and mixed with blood. I stood and looked in the mirror, and then I saw the blood mixed with the sweat disappearing as if it were not there at all. And then I knew, like I had always believed, that all this was real because it happened to me and the flame he gave to me in the dream. It's been inside me all along, and it's inside you, for all you have to do is believe.

OUR SPIRIT

In these nice, warm days of spring when you forget about the freezing cold of winter, we go out and clean up the mess that winter's left behind. We weed and mow the lawn, plant and water the flowers until it's perfect in your eyes. Then you sit back and enjoy the beauty that you help bring to life.

The same goes for life itself. We're born, and then we must be tended to from that seed until we're in full bloom and beyond. So in life itself we are born. We grow up and become old and then we die. We have a second chance to be reborn again after we die in this life. It's simple but it's not. First you have to believe in someone that you have never seen. Yet something tells you he is there, something deep, deep down inside, for when you think about it, it wants to come alive. It's the spirit. It's speaking to you; you have never seen it. Yet you know it's been with you all your life. You just have to say yes, and it will come alive. It's in all of us, this spirit.

God is the one we have never seen, and yet our spirit belongs to him. It's a part of him. It's been with him before the beginning of time, and yes, he wants it back, this spirit that's inside of us.

That's why he sent his Son who died for us. So that in time when our bodies die, our spirit lives on through his Son forevermore, and that's a long, long time.

All you have to do is call upon the son's name and truly believe.

And then you can live with the Father and his Son in their kingdom forevermore. Yes, forevermore, and that's a long, long, long time.

JUSTIFY THE MEANS

Throughout our history, the history of mankind, man has waged war at one another from the beginning until now and probably beyond. Spilling blood from both sides, yes, spreading it all around. These wars, these battles, no matter how big or small, do they justify the means? Do they do justice for all? In some cases, yes. In some cases, no. In the Bible, the Hebrews did battle as directed through the prophets. That was direct from God. Rather they understood it or not. They did it without question, for it was directly from God. David did battle and shed a lot of blood. But through God, he united his people and made them all as one under God. Throughout the ages, from David on down, war has been waged, battles were fought, lives were lost; and in the end, only one side won. But to what means? We fought for our independence. It took a few years and we won. We fought a Civil War; one side won. It brought about a better nation far beyond our wildest dreams. We fought other wars, World War I and II.

Those wars were the bloodiest and deadliest this world has ever seen. It brought peace and independence to countries and its people that never existed until then. So why do we fight? Why do we wage war? Are we still as barbaric as our ancestors were?

One man becomes a dictator. His country is very, very small. Or one idea that says, "Do it our way or your heads will fall." We are a civilized people. Yes, sometimes we must take a stand; stand up to the tyrants and give the people a hand. Help them out no matter if their faith is different than ours. As in war, mistakes are made, so we must learn from those mistakes and never let them happen again once the war is over and our job is complete. We must give those people their independence, their rights to choose. Will we, or will they repeat the same thing from the past? So we all must remember those bad and terrible things, those things that we did in the past, from the stories in the Bible to slavery in our own countries past. From the Holocaust that tried to annihilate a people because of a name or who they are to the dictator of Iraq and the Taliban in Afghanistan to the regions of Darfur and maybe somewhere else today or beyond.

We as a people, as citizens of the world, this is the only home we have. Let's keep it in one piece and trust each other with respect. Help each other out, and when a dictator or an idea arises and it puts the people in harm's way or to the brink of extinction, then we as a world must stand up and take a stand. And help justify those means to the end.

JUDGING ALL

Christians throughout the world celebrate Easter as the holiest day of the year, but what does it mean to the believers and nonbelievers alike that confrontation has been going on for two thousand years and will still continue until finally the truth will be unveiled? And when that day comes, only God knows what will happen to us that believe and to those that do not. There has to be some truth to all this. If not, then Jesus died on the cross without a cause. But if we read the Good Book and read it right, we read in Jeremiah, and Jeremiah says it right. He, Jesus, was born in this world for one purpose. That purpose was to die on the cross for us all, to die for those back then, for us today, for our children's children that is to come until that day when he judges us all.

For those that believe, as he said, are reborn again. Not of the flesh, but of the spirit, and it will be tough to live such a life, but his spirit's with us. Through all your ups and downs he will carry you 100 percent of the time. To the unbelievers, if their work here on earth is just and right, he will judge them for that, and that he gives his word to me. That's all right, for there are many mansions there, so he has foretold maybe one for each of us. But for me it does not matter as long as I am there, sitting at his table forever and evermore, for we cannot judge each other because of our different beliefs.

For he said, "Judge not, for ye shall be judged. For I will judge, and I will judge all by the works they have done on earth, and I will judge them fair and judge them with truth, for I am truth, and I am right. To those that truly believe and follow after me, their sins have been washed by my blood, and they shall not be judged but shall pass free to my kingdom forevermore." For as a song we used to sing when I was a kid, you go to your church, and I'll go to mine, but let's walk the road together. Our fathers built them side by side, so let's hold hands and walk there together, for there is but one church as there is but one God. And through his Son, this Jewish Messiah, this Jesus the Christ, we as a people can all overcome and make this earth a better place until he comes and sits on the throne of David and rule us all with truth and with pure love for us all.

CHANGE THE PAST

Just a quick thought. What would you do if you had the chance to go back to a certain time and see history unfold and you see the truth as it unfolds? What day? What year? Do you have one in mind? Would it be Dallas or Peral? Or even at the beginning of time? How far back would you go to set the record straight? And when you get back, you tell what you have seen, and it's not at all what the history books cut it out to be. Would the people you tell believe you, or would they say you're insane? If you could go back in time—and yes, time will only tell—would you go back and change that wrong and make it right, no matter how far back in time you go? Would you, or do you have the right to change history and adjust it to make it so? And if you do and come back, what will your time look like, or will you even be around? Take World War II. That's not that far back. Would you kill Hitler as a baby? Would that make the wrong, right? He's just a baby as innocent as can be. In God's eyes, you killed a child no matter what he would grow up to be.

If World War II didn't happen after what you just did, what would the world be like when you return to your own time? Millions died in World War II. Or would there be someone else to take Hitler's place and be worse? And just maybe he would almost destroy the human race, for you see, when you change history—no matter how big or small—the world as you knew it would not be the same at all.

Just suppose the ones that died in World War II were alive and no World War II happened at all. Still, the future would have changed. For millions and millions in your time would not have been born at all.

Maybe someone in your family died and you wanted them to still be around, so you change history to suit yourself, and look—just look at what you did to time. We have all thought of this at some time or another. We cannot, or should not, go back to change the wrong and make it right. For ours is today and tomorrow—let the past stay in the past. But remember it. Yes, remember it, so we don't repeat it again, so things must stay the way they are. We can change today for a better tomorrow, look at our past, and remember it. And if it's bad, we can't change it, for it already happened. We can read it as history today. We can make sure it doesn't happen again, so we can make a better tomorrow.

ARE WE AS FOOLISH AS THEM?

I bow my head in silence, wondering what it was like living back when the prophets would talk to the angels, receiving messages through them from God. It must have been a hard life, for a lot of those messages were of doom.

The king or the people had done wrong. They turned their backs on the most high.

Are we as a people living today doing the same thing but in a different way? We say we believe in God. But we take prayer out of our schools—no Ten Commandments in our public buildings or our courts. Are we as foolish as them?

We pledge allegiance to our flag. We serve our country with pride; then further on, we say we are one nation under God. Are we going to say farewell to that as well?

We are a great nation, the greatest the world has ever seen. We believe and say one nation under God. But to a few, even that's gone too far. The Hebrews went and worshipped a false god—the god's name was Baal, and God punished them. Are we, as a people, becoming as foolish as them?

Can you imagine, if you can, this nation, our country, without mentioning the word *God*? Would we be where we are today? Would we have the freedom to say the things we say we are not? We are not a perfect country, nor are we a perfect people. We come from every part of this planet. Every religion and some no religion. This country, our country, was founded by our forefathers—our constitution says we the people, one nation under God. So think it over, for deep down inside, we know this nation cannot survive without the belief in God.

Then we can smile and say his name. For then we know we won't be as foolish as them.

MAN AND HIS ACHIEVEMENTS

In the beginning, a time long, long ago, between four rivers, a garden did grow. In the garden the owner, with his mind or the wave of his hand, planted all manner of life, including man. He told the man to tend to all. Name the beast, the birds, name them all. We have heard this story from the time when we were young, the story about Eden, the serpent, and the downfall of mankind. But God created man in his own image; in his own in image he created man. God said, "I will let man live, but sin shall follow him no matter where he goes and lives." And the serpent followed man from that time until now, planning and plotting the downfall of mankind.

Now man has achieved wonders from the time he was put up on the ground, wonders upon wonders from cities that reach into the sky. To cars, trucks, trains that move across the ground. Using his thought, man has achieved a lot, from curing diseases of all kinds to feeding people around the world one basket at a time and scientists looking out into the heavens. And what do they see? Billions of galaxies and trillions of stars and planets in each. And with their telescopes, they see wonders of the universe that's never been seen before. Yes, galaxies like ours but a million times larger. They say it's beyond their belief, the size, the scope, and it's still growing even more so as I speak.

For we—humans or mankind, for that's what we are called—will explore the universe if God is willing, one day at a time. We have put man on the moon, a great achievement far beyond what our ancestors believed. Man has done a great deal from his early times. He can fly around the world in a very, very short time. Now he speaks and sees someone in a box at the same time even though they are twenty-four hours apart. We tend to our young and to our old. We help out the needy when crises arise, wherever they be. We believe and pray to God in our own special way, and above all, we need God every second of the day. And that serpent, he's still around, feeding man with hate and spreading it all around. It spreads like no other disease. It's called greed, envy, and hate. You know you see and feel it every day, and it's been around from the beginning until now and beyond.

So with all the advancement man has achieved, no achievement is far greater than what God has given thee, to love one another as he has loved you. And when that happens, and it will in the end, he will banish the serpent and his followers forevermore. He will sit on his throne and rule the world with love. Until then, be watchful, for God is looking down on us from above.

THE EARTH

It was a cold, cold wintery night, and the stars were out very, very bright. As I looked up, I saw that they were there blinking back at me. And I smiled with great delight, wondering if there was one out there that may be like me. I am old. Very old, older than the river and seas, older than the living things that live on and inside and above me. I was created in the beginning, and in the beginning, he created me with the molding of his hands or just his thought he created me. He created me from atoms he brought from far, far away. Like all the other bodies in the heavens, he created them in the same manner as me. Then he placed me in a dark and cold, cold place, and his thought came to me, and said, "I must do something to this darkness, for without it nothing can see."

And he took some atoms and made a ball of yellow light and placed it in the heavens far. But not that far away from me, and this ball of light he called it the sun. Then he divided this darkness into two parts. He called the light day and the darkness night. And the light, it warmed me, and I started to grow. I was happy, so I spun around and around this ball of light that he called the sun. It felt good and warm, and as time passed, I changed—I was young. And being young, I grew, and my face changed many times: some parts cold, some not, some a warm perfect spot. I was in one piece all round, one piece of solid ground. Then again I changed—my face split and came apart. Why, I don't know. Then I started to cry. As I cried, I filled the spaces.

He came and said, "This looks good." He called my solid places land, and my tears he called seas. He smiled and said, "This was good." And I changed more over the eons of time. He made me grow more, pushing parts of me up to touch the heavens. He called them mountains; the low he called valleys and fertile ground. As more time passed, he sowed what he said was seed. My tears he put life in what's now called the sea. On solid ground the seed grew into grass, trees, and vines that bore what he called fruit and grain, and that was fine. He created and put on me beast of the earth, fish of the sea, and fowl of the air. He told me it was good; then he created male and female. He said they were the likeness of himself and told me they will have dominion over all that there is.

Yes, this male and female, they were different than the beast and fowl. They had thought, could speak, and could take care of their young. After eons and eons of time, they moved from place to place and covered my entire face. Now I see things they built. They took from me the earth and made what they call cities, roads, and more. They made moving things that run on my face and things that fly like the fowl through the sky. And my face and tears they fill with their waste that pollutes everything in my face and tears, even the air. Then I see a few, so very few helping to restore my face and clean up my tears. I ask why they are doing this to me; then as I look up and see all the heavens aglow, one comes to me and says, "Soon he will come again. He will make you new or whole." I ask him when. He says, "I cannot tell you when. You and the heavens will be made new or whole. For only he, the Father, knows the day and the hour, and then everything will be new.

I am the earth, and these are things he said to me, and yes, they are true.

DECEMBER 21, 2012

In every culture and religion, it's been said time and time again that the world will live then die, then live again. From the earliest writings in China to the Mayan calendar to the Native Americans and others, it is said that December 21, 2012 is the time once again for the earth to die and be born again. That's what they have all written down from three thousand years in the past up to the modern times. Something is going to happen on that date. What will happen, the truth is, we don't know. The sun will be at the center of our galaxy. This happens once every twenty-six thousand years or so.

Will we, as a planet, be torn apart? Will the earth's poles shift a little or shift a lot, if it happens as some scientists predict? Earth is in a lot of trouble, and yes, that's saying a heck of a lot. In the Good Book, it states that the sun will go black, that wormwood will fall. The rivers will turn bloodred, mountains will shake, and islands will disappear according to John. But John doesn't give a date, and if we don't know, then how can we be prepared? For most of us, we in the modern and electronic age, we don't know how to plant crops and live off the land like our forefathers did not so long ago. Will the oceans rise so high it will cover the cities by the shore? Will the mountains flatten where they used to be tall? Will there be earthquakes and volcanoes where there were no faults at all? Who is to be safe no matter where they live? Millions will be displaced, and millions more will cease to live, for they will already be dead. Is this just a fairy tale? For no one knows when the end will be.

Time and again, this has happened to the earth in the past. Maybe it will happen as they say, and just maybe God will let it go away. For the last book in the Good Book tells things that's similar but in a different way. I believe in the Good Book, and it will happen in God's way on that day, and only God knows the day and hour. So things will happen on this earth time and again. We must be prepared in a different way, for he says he will come back. That day we know not when. I believe something may happen on that day that may affect us all. But the end of life as we know it, I don't believe it at all. For only God knows that day and hour, not the Mayan, nor the seers, nor the scientists as they would predict. Perhaps if anything happens on that date as the Mayan calendar and others would say, it will affect the whole earth, not just here or there. So be prepared and go about your daily chore and ask God for forgiveness and mercy. And just maybe, yes maybe, he will let us live a little while longer here on this planet we call earth.

DREAMS

Dreams, we all have had them. Some are called daydreams when you sit down during the day and make those dreams up. We still do. Same as when we were still kids, those invisible friends we played with, those types of dreams we could control, and those other dreams—those that came to us while we were in bed asleep. You know somewhere between being awake and sleep, some we don't remember at all, others we just a glimpse, and that's all. It's those other dreams, some good, some bad. The good ones, you wake up and feel fine, and you smile and say those dreams were fine. But those other dreams, those dreams that make you roll and toss then scream. You wake up with a cold sweat, afraid to go back to sleep. Then there are other dreams good and bad. You wake up then go back to sleep; it's like watching TV. It continues all night until finally in the morning you wake up, get out of bed, but those still linger in your head.

We see and do things during the day or watch something on TV. Then we dream about it after we go to sleep. The Good Book says in those days we shall see visions and dreams, dreams yes. They have been around since the beginning. Then there are dreams, other dreams. Remember Jacob and his ladder? Was it true that he wrestled with an angel afterward and that he became lame? Just maybe that dream was true. Then pharaoh of Egypt, he dreamed of seven fat cows and seven skinny cows or lean cows. And the seven lean cows ate the seven fat cows. What did it mean and it take Joseph to interpret those dreams of seven years of plenty, seven years of drought? That dream came true, so dreams, yes, they have been around for a long time.

My mom, God bless her heart, she had dreams, and they came true. She dreamed of a time back at the beginning of World War II. Mom was from the hills of Kentucky. She didn't know the insignias of any country, maybe not even her own. She had two sons in the army. She was in the hospital with me. I was nine days old. That night, or should I say early in the morning, she had a dream, a sad dream. But she didn't know. She saw mountains reaching high into the sky, a beautiful land and a harbor with lots of ships below waiting for the first ray of the morning sun.

As she watched, she saw planes, quite a few coming over those mountains that stood high in the sky, with a red ball on their tails that shined brightly against the morning sun. Then something happened as if all hell broke loose. Those planes went down dropping bombs. All she could see were bodies floating in the water, some dressed in white, some in blue, some nothing at all. She watched as lots of those ships went down below the waves. Then the planes left and flew away. She started screaming. The nurses and the doctor on duty came running to calm her down. She told them of the dream and what happened. After they calmed her down, they said she was thinking of her sons. Then a few hours later, the news came on of what my mother saw. It came true. They kept it from her, for she just had her twelfth child—a son—me.

That day we will never forget. That day will live in infamy, December 7, 1941. Many years later, while I was watching TV with Mom, we were watching a movie about December 7, 1941. Mom stood up and pointed at the TV. She said, "That's what I saw, those mountains, those planes and ships and the bodies of those men." Then she sat down and cried. I comforted her, told her God gave her that dream for a reason, and only God knows why. My dad was coal miner, and yes, he also had a steel during those early years way before World War II. Dad moonshined, that's called white lighting, to help keep his family alive. Then one day, Mom asked Dad how many barrels he had on the ridge. He replied three. She looked at him and said, "I had a dream last night. I saw two on fire rolling down the ridge toward the house."

Dad didn't like Mom's dreams. Yet he knew what the Bible said about them. He told her to get back in the house; then he went upon that mountain that Mom called a ridge. Lo and behold, two barrels exploded sometime during the night. They both told me this and said it was true. Dad never explained why he didn't want to know anything about dreams. So I believe in dreams or visions. John of Patmos saw visions and wrote it down. From Nostradamus five hundred years ago to Edgar Casey and others, they did likewise have dreams. Visions have been around for some time. Are we living in those days that John speaks about? About your young men, they shall dream dreams; your old will see visions. Are we at that time that the Mayan calendar says it's right? Truth is, only God knows. So are they real, or make-believe visions?

On the other hand, if we knew what the visions were and what they meant, we might be able to change the outcome from bad to good. Visions are given to us for a purpose, to change something maybe before it happens. Truth is, we will never know. Regarding the visions, some say "you're nuts," while others will say, "tell me, let's figure this out." To me, visions are there for a purpose: to act, hope, and pray to change what was shown from wrong to right. Dreams are dreams. Mostly that's all there is. A few, yes, very few when you dream those, you will know, for it will stay in your head and not go away. Those dreams are left up to you—you can act on them or not.

Remember a dream that you had, and then it came true. You're afraid to tell someone, afraid of what they might do, so you keep it to yourself. Dreams you must decide, like Mom's she told, by that time it was too late, even if they told would anyone believe, maybe if it were by a famous person but, Mom, a coal miner's wife I doubt it. So dreams, why do we have them? Are they part of life? I've heard people say if we don't dream, we die. To me that's hearsay. Do they have a meaning, a purpose in life? The Bible has a few of those dreams and visions, and yes, they came true, but in the end only God knows. So dream your dreams, and if you have a vision and are wide awake, pray to God first. Ask him to help you through it—he may be testing you. Best of all, take that vision, and take it on faith. You must use your own judgment, and then you may ask why these visions happen. I don't know; I'm not God. All I can say is that the truth is God, and only God knows the meaning to these dreams and visions and to life itself.

THE OLD MAN IN THE CITY

As he walks the city in broad daylight with the tall glass buildings shining so bright and the inhabitants going to and fro, some walking fast, some walking slow, he looks into their eyes, and they stare back, some bright and some with a smile that's a delight. The others that he sees, their eyes say it all. Despair, nowhere to go or to be. If he asked them, would they tell him? Or would they just say "I don't know" and go about their own way? He looks over and sees a newsstand. The headlines read that Wall Street collapses and the market is in ruin. Then they say we're in a down spin, but to others they turn, snub those and walk away. They enter those tall glass buildings where they work, live, and play. They made money selling stocks, bonds, and they inflated the market so that they could stay in those glass buildings, thinking they would never leave, making millions of dollars off the people like those that they see. Then they tell the media, "It's not my fault that my company went broke," putting thousands of people out of work and onto the streets, many with families, others by themselves standing in soup lines to nourish their bodies back to good health.

They have never done this before as he heard them say, standing in lines for a handout. What else can happen to us this day? As they stand in the bread lines waiting on something to eat, one old man, tall and lean, who hadn't had a bath in weeks, stands in line and looks at them with a grin. "I will tell you," he said as he looked at them with a straight and somber face. "I've been here before in lines small and large for many years. If it were you, you might even forget. It happened then, it's happening now. Greedy people from Main Street to Wall Street lining their pockets with millions of your dollars while saying it's not their fault, it's just the way the market grows and falls, but pay me those millions, we signed a contract, it's legal, even if thousands are laid off and the company folds. So they lined their pockets with all that cash. While a lot that have been laid off have to look through other people's trash to stay alive."

The old man looked at the people and said, with those eyes that bind you, you cannot look away, "I have been here a long time, much longer than time even knows. I've seen it all from close up and afar. This greed, it follows man wherever he goes." There is another side to this ordeal as they looked at the old man and stared into his eyes. Smiles came on their faces and tears in their eyes; they knew what he meant as they saw him fade away. They held hands, knelt, and began to pray. He smiled as he walked away. He gave them faith and hope like so many other times in days gone by, for he will be with them all the time. And those of greed, they will answer, and it will be to him on that day. But for now, this lesson is hard and cold, but turn the page and start anew. Set aside your differences just as the ones that listened to the old man. Open your hearts and minds; help those that are in need. And if you ask and it's sincere, then perhaps that old man will again reappear.

THE RAIN

On a warm sunny afternoon, not a cloud in the sky, and the temperature was reaching a little high. You go outside with the hopes of getting a tan. Then out of nowhere it started to rain. As you looked up, no clouds to form the rain were in the sky. Then it stopped, and you looked around—not a drop of water was on the ground. This is wrong; it can't be right. Nothing like this can happen—this much water, it can't evaporate that fast. The more you look, the more you wonder, "Did I imagine this? If so, I wonder why." Then you put it past you, and you lay down for that tan. You close your eyes, and to your surprise, it happens all over again. You are totally soaken wet; then you get up and you're dry. This is getting a little weird, so you go back inside. As you sit and look outside, you wonder why it rained then it went dry. You have not heard of this before, so you call the weather station. You get nothing, for even they don't know why. "Am I going nuts, or am I already insane" Then you look out again, and it's starts to rain. "What's going on?" you ask yourself. And without knowing it, you sit down and start to cry.

Then the rain stops, and the sun comes out. The brightness of the sun is so bright. You even see it in the house, but the warmth that was inside was totally different than the warmth that stayed outside. "I don't believe any of this." Then a voice said, "Why then did you cry?" As he opened his eyes, he could see someone so bright, but it didn't hurt his eyes. And the voice said, "You mock people, you shame them for their beliefs, and yet deep inside you're hurting. Would you like to know why? Look all around you, your home, your car, your job, you have it all. All the power money can buy. You can have it all, and then at the end you lose something you don't believe in, you lose your soul. The rain that fell and then dried up, that's your life in three—you are born, you grow up, and then you die.

"Where do you go from there? Would you like to be reborn and give it another try? You went to church when you were a kid. You read of John the Baptist. He baptized with water, for water is life. He even baptized me. I give eternal life, if only you believe. Many believe and call on my name. You can be reborn but not of the flesh but of the spirit. Then you can, after this life, have eternal life with me." And you fall down, and your life comes back to you before your eyes. You ask for forgiveness, and the voice says, "I will forgive in a twinkle of an eye." And you open your eyes; everything felt fresh and new. The voice and light has gone, but his spirit stayed inside of you. For you know what you saw, but no one would believe. But to those that know you, they know you have totally changed. And as you smile and speak, that spirit goes forth to someone else, and when that rain falls, it just might fall on you.

THE DECEIVER

In a time, it does not matter where or when, man has walked the earth from the beginning time and again. From the beginning until now, man has toiled upon the ground. And back in time and maybe now, one with a strong fist and a firm loud shout, one man from that crowd will stand out. He puts into bondage and into chains men, women, and children. To him, they're all the same. He puts into their minds and into their hearts of war and hate, and in the end it's all the same. The stench of death in its place, oh yes, we know this man of hate. He's been around ever since the time in the garden when he was put to crawl upon the ground. And since that time, he's put into men's hearts that same old thing of war and hate. He's the liar of all liars and thief of all thieves. He will deceive you in ways he only knows how, for his message is to destroy all, and he doesn't care how.

He'll play up to the kingdoms, countries, and realms for a while. Then he will let them fall screaming, screaming as they come tumbling down, for he and his demons that followed him here, they tried the same thing in heaven. Now they are doing it here. A war in heaven, it's hard to believe. But that's what God said, and it's in the Bible. All you have to do is pick up the Bible and read. He could have destroyed them with a wave of his hand or just a thought, and they would be gone from his sight. But a plan he has for them, and it won't be till the end. He will put into men's hearts one that is the comforter, and all man has to do is ask, and the evil one shall part. But he is the deceiver of all times. Yes, he will try to deceive again and again, so it will be.

As time goes on, with wars and rumors of wars, he will try to make it last. Then one day, they will come to show men here on earth that God's word will be done. They are the two witnesses. I know not their names; they will have the power of heaven, and they will do as he demands, for they have the power direct from God to see if man will change in their hearts and their minds. Some will change and sing a song, a song to God 144,000 strong. But a lot will not. The witnesses will fall; he will kill them both, like others that believe so many times before, and let the world see them fall as people trample over them in the streets and give gifts to one another because what the witnesses had done to them.

And after three days lying in the street, God will raise them up into heaven, and all the world shall see. Then the battle of all battles will begin, and it will be at that place called Armageddon. How long it will last, I don't know. A second, a year, a hundred years or more? Only God knows, but until that time, he gives us signs, those signs that John wrote down for us to see and hear. So be prepared and wait. Set aside these evil thoughts of greed, envy, and hate and look toward the heavens. Pray and wait for God. Yes, God has been here all along and will still be here long after he has gone. So read the book written by John. Yes, that book, the one everyone talks about, the last one in that book, that holy book. All you have to do is read it and ask him for help. All you have to do is open your door to your heart, and he will come in, this comforter, and be with you past judgment and beyond in his kingdom. As he said, "I will create a new heaven and a new earth, you shall be my people, and I your God, and I will rule you all, with pure truth and love for one and all. And the deceiver and those that follow him, I shall remove them and remember them no more. And you my chosen shall be with me forevermore."

THE DECEIVER AND
THE TWIN TOWERS

He walks this city from one end to the other, smiling to himself as he watches the people from all walks of life going to and from their place of work. As he walks, he keeps looking up, waiting for something to happen. Soon he stands in front of two magnificent buildings. They are just alike, they're called the Twin Towers, the towers that stand out from all the rest. Tall and straight, you can see them from afar, home to lots of companies, where thousands of people come and go. It's like a city in a city, these towers standing mighty tall and straight. He looks and he sees the people entering them on this bright September 11 day. So he thinks to himself as he looks toward the east high in the sky. He smiles with great delight as he watches two planes take off and fly toward the western sky.

Soon, real soon, he will see and hear the screaming, the crying, the rumble that will fill this city. The people will ask and wonder why. No one can see him, for we all know who he is. He's been around before the beginning of time. We know him by many names. In the end, those names, they're all the same. He puts into men's hearts this greed, envy, and hate. To some he hardens their heart, makes them do his will. He's getting even one way or another. A payback for when he was exiled to earth. He will continue on and on until that day he is put permanently in his place. Then he looks up, smiles with delight, and he leans against the towers. He's also far away to see the carnage up close and afar.

Then that time has come. Two planes, they slam into the towers. As the planes hit the towers one after the other and explode, the planes that are full of fuel cause an inferno so hot that it melts the steel. Then those buildings, those beautiful twins, they collapse, leaving thousands of people dead. Thousands more are hurt from the blast and debris. Children without their parents, husbands without their wives. Terrorists all of them, and the innocent as well, they all on that September 11 day, they all lost their lives.

He looks at the scene as the building came tumbling down. He cries out to himself with great delight. "This has made my day. In my world, I have gained nineteen more souls. They thought they were doing the right thing, these terrorists. Yes, now they are mine forevermore." It will take years to clean up the mess and to rebuild.

To those that survived and the families of those that lost their lives, there is someone above. He is holding out his arms, receiving the ones that lost their lives, taking them to the other side to be with him in a place called paradise. Two other planes crashed that day, killing all on board. The terrorists will be with their comrades in a place we call hell. The others, the innocents, will join those from the twins and be with them in paradise on the other side. This beast, this Satan, he will do this again and again, deceiving people until that time when he is held responsible. That will only be in the end. Until that time, we must take a better stand. We must stand up, help each other, put aside this greed, envy, and hate. No matter who or what we are, we must all stand up united against this common foe. Pray to God above in your own religious way. Read the Good Book, the last one written by John; then go to your place of worship and pray. Then on that day, that great judgment day, we will be redeemed. And

Satan, those that followed him, will be cast aside in that lake with no escape forevermore. We the innocent, those that truly believe will be with God in paradise, yes, paradise, That's on the other side forevermore.

SATAN

He walks the land both day and night, waiting and watching for that moment when things are just right. He plots and plans on the things he wants man to do, by putting a notion, an idea into their minds and their hearts. He wants to make them his own right from the very start. He's been doing this from the beginning, down through the eons of time and down to the present and even beyond. Yes, he tried to overthrow heaven and was cast out. He and his angels were cast out into the earth. Then he says, "I will get even." He did it to Eve, and that was the start.

So down through the ages, he did his will. From the garden to the flood and beyond still, he put lust into David's heart and blood on his hands. He tempted the Son and showed him the world. The Son rebuked him. He left and bothered him no more, and by entering Judas, Judas betrayed the Son for thirty pieces of silver, which led the Son to his death. He must have thought, "This is it, this is the end. I've beaten heaven. I'm as strong or stronger than them." But the Son arose and ascended to his Father. So now he knows the war has not ended, and he had not won. So now he pulls out everything. He's got to make mankind wage war against one another until that time, and only God knows when the Son will come on a horse as a warrior with all the angels of heaven to face Satan for the last time and the last battle for mankind. He knows this is the big one and he will lose it all, but he will take as many as he can, for that mark on their forehead or the palm of their hand tells it all, along with his angels. They will be cast in the lake forever and ever, with no way to escape, and God will remember them no more. And he and his Son will set up a new kingdom in a new heaven and earth. He will rule his people, his flock with total love forevermore. Until that time, we must keep the faith and avoid this greed, envy, and this hate and trust in God and his Son. For they, yes, they know best.

Why? Because they, God and his Son, Jesus, have been around way before the beginning of time itself. Remember, they are the first and the last, and this Satan knows that. He knows his days here are numbered. And yes, he will take as many as he can. So the bottom line to this is that it's left up to you.

PART TWO

GOD AND COUNTRY

GOD AND COUNTRY

Down in the valley where the tall green grass grows, where my forefathers settled many, many years ago, they came from the old country, England, to be precise, looking for a better and a richer life. It was hard starting from scratch, with only a few clothes and some tools in a sack. But they were good craftsmen. They brought their tools and their know-how, and that's how it began. Other families came, some had money, others nothing, not a penny to their name. Just hope and a dream. That's what they all wanted to fulfill.

They started in the East and moved to the South and West. They gained their freedom, yes, at a great cost. Over the years, they grew and became great, stretching from the Atlantic to the Pacific; and yes, along the way, they did make mistakes. From the trails of tears, slavery, and other things we had to endure. Then our eyes opened, yes, again at a great cost. Men in blue and men in gray fighting each other, some fighting and not knowing what they were fighting for. But in the end, the country reunited and faced up to all that shame. They held hands and rebuilt what they had destroyed. While others still stuck to the old ways and refused to conform at all. Now it's been many a year since. The war between the states, we have become a mighty and powerful nation, none like the world has seen. We're trying to make things right, but things keep popping up. Like kids or our pets, they sometimes go astray, and in the past decade or so, we have went astray so far this time. We may be lost, according to some. Yet we have come a long, long way, even setting foot on the moon and beyond. But for now, we must get down to basics, get back down to earth, help the sick, the poor, help each other by lending a hand.

We have done it in the past. We can do it again by trusting and believing in each other. And above all, we must trust and believe in God. Without our faith in him, where would we be now? Would we have all the freedoms we take for granted? Would we still be a land of liberty with freedom for all? We must stop and think where we would be if we never used the phrase "in God we trust" at all, for God gave our forefathers the insight to form this country out of nothing. And with those other words, "one nation under God with liberty and justice for all," would we still have that today if we didn't trust in God?

This is something to think about. But for me, we would be nothing. Like we are today if we didn't believe in God.

Believe in God and ask him for help. And in time, little by little, he will hear our prayer like so many times in the past; and he, by us believing in him, will save this country. And we pray he will save us all.

All we have to do is truly believe. And trust in God.

OUR COUNTRY CAN BE FIXED

I stand on a mountaintop so high, so high I could touch the sky. As I look out across this vast land of ours, from the north to the south, from the east to the west, I see the beauties and the wonders at their very best. From the snow peaks of the Rockies to the deserts and rivers far below. To the cornfields in Iowa, standing tall row after row. To the wheat fields of the Dakotas, amber and blowing in the wind. The apples of Washington to Napa valley and the farms that feed our nation days on end. We have Idaho and its potatoes, Texas and its beef. Florida has its oranges, and Georgia has its peaches.

From all over this vast country of ours, farmers large and small feed everyone here, and a lot goes abroad. From small towns to large cities, we all have our own style and decor. We're from every country in the world, different races, different beliefs. We all come here for a better life, from the pilgrims down to the newest ones off the boat. To pledge allegiance and say one nation under God, and this nation, with so many from all walks of life, still gives us hope. We are a people. We must rise and take a stand against corruption that leads to greed, envy, and hate. For we as a nation, we must put this all aside and stand up together as one to help each other to get our country back on the right track, to rebuild our factories and mills from the rust belts of the Great Lakes to the delta and the gulf. Put Americans back to work, for I know we are the best the world has got. For they have closed our factories and mills and put people out of work and built overseas just to make a huge profit off the people like you and me. This country has gone down the tubes in the last ten years or so, but it has been building up for thirty years or more. It's not a simple solution. It can't be fixed by one man alone. We must pull together as a people and put our differences aside, join together as one; then the world can look at us again and say that's the America that was.

Until that time, we must have faith in our country, our people, and our pride. Stand up and say, "Yes, oh yes, we can." For we now have each other and are holding each other's hand. We can rebuild this great country of ours like our forefathers did by the sweat of their brow and the blood from their hands and trust in the one that created us. Trust in him. Remember that God has never left our side; we left him. Now by praying to him and trusting in each other, then we can truly say yes, America, yes, we can.

CITY AND COUNTRY

He walks through the city in daylight and at night, checking things out and making sure it's all right. From the streets that are flashing with neon signs to the alleys that are dark, dingy with the stench that's thrown all around. He sees the high-rises where the rich live and play, to the ghettos where dealers sell their drugs twenty-four hours a day. He sees the people down and depressed with layoffs and downsizing. To them, no help is on the way. He walks by the shelters that put the homeless up for the night. He sees the volunteers who help both through the day and night. He sees people helping out people both great and small. Some giving a little, some a lot. And to them that give, it does matter. It matters a lot.

He sees houses all boarded up on the streets that he walks, with signs saying "No trespassing or entering, for that's the law," while people go homeless throughout the land. The banks receive billions in a bailout. Still they don't lend a hand. From city to city, he has seen it all. This economic downturn, it will affect us all. The government will help and push for more aid. Some say we're not doing enough. Others we have gone too far. Both sides of the aisle, they bicker. To them there's no middle ground. From the president all the way down, they must work together to turn this country around and to stop excessive spending and the excessive pay.

So turn to each other, both rich and poor and anywhere in between. Help each other, for you are a proud people and you're strong. For if not, you will all suffer in the end. Don't be ashamed to pray and ask for help, for he's been around. Yes, he knows what it's all about. To love one another as he has loved you, and you shall be glorious again. Yes, it may take time. He will be here. He never goes away, for it is you, like the lost sheep, you go astray.

And as the good shepherd tends his flock, for this greed, envy, and hate has no place. And once they are erased, America, you will see and again fill his grace.

AMERICA, STAND UP

He stands and looks at this great nation of ours, sees many great things from close up and from afar. From the great Atlantic to the wide Pacific and its shores. From the high peaks of the Rockies to the deserts far below, from the Great Lakes to where the Mississippi flows, to the corn and wheat fields of Iowa and Dakotas from the Ohio valley to the Blue Ridge Mountains. He looks out across this vast country of ours and sees things that should not be: high rise in unemployment, people losing their jobs and homes. Where millions of them walk the streets, their families by their side, he looks into their eyes. He sees despair, no hope to be found anywhere. They have given up, their lifelong savings down the drain.

Then his mind and eyes go to that city where the marble buildings shine brightly in the noonday sun. He goes to a place called Capitol Hill, then the White House where the people's leader works and lives. He listens to both sides. They're saying it's better to do it their way, for they know what's wrong. If they knew what was wrong, this country would not be in this mess, and it would be going strong. The people would still have their jobs and homes. So the government that represents the people gave billions to finance companies and banks to stimulate the economy to get back on its feet, but instead what did they was throw lavish outings and large pay raises and bonuses to their CEOs for a great job. Yes, a great job not so well done.

He looks at them and shakes his head. Yes, he knows, and the truth speaks for itself. Greed is the root of all evil, and envy follows close behind. For envy wants more than greed. With that, it leads to a threesome. Both will hate to get what they want. They joined forces and combined this greed, envy, and hate, for it's been around for a mighty long time, so they take their millions while putting millions out on the street. Now the government owns over 50 percent of the companies they bailed out. Then the country has the last say about who gets what and how much, for if the companies from Wall Street on down were doing a great job, they would still be on solid ground. The stockholders gave them their OK; now they want more. Why? So they can give themselves extra bonuses in pay.

Most should be fired from the CEOs on down, even to the members of the board, without bailouts, stock options, or anything in between. Then put someone in charge, no pay higher than one million, no bonuses, perks, or stocks. They get the same benefits as the workers at the mill get fired if they don't do their job. They can stand in the unemployment line and draw food stamps just like the ones they fired. A company that's publicly owned, that's all they get, and nothing more—they pay for everything else just like the workers. Put this country and its people first. Even in these hard times, he still knows they give more to the needy around the world than a lot of countries combined. The people, they are strong. They will survive. Now it's time to give back to its people, homes at a lower rate, then jobs. Make it the law. No closing of factories to build abroad; build them here till this country and the world gets on even scale. Put greed, envy, and hate far, far, far behind and start anew from Wall Street to Main Street, from the White House to Capitol Hill.

Put our politics aside and stand as Americans. Yes, America, we can be proud. Instead of saying "God bless America" as we usually do, we should reverse that saying and say, "America, bless God, for he has blessed this country from the start. He blesses it yet still from close-up and afar, for he looks out across this land. He sees the greatness that's within. Then we can stand up together, look up to him, then we can say, "Yes, America, with his help, yes, we can."

REBUILD AMERICA

How many times have you heard people say, "If I were wealthy and rich, it would be done my way"? Yes, we have all said it at one time or another. Rather, we were born in wealth or made it the old-fashioned way. To a lot, the more they have, the more they want. But to others that give back, they don't ask for anything in return. The same goes for countries all around the world. Some will give a little, some a lot. Of all the countries, America gives the most. When catastrophes hit, no matter where it's at, Americans dig deep into their pockets to help no matter where it's at. From schoolkids collecting nickels and dimes to the elderly and others on a fixed income, they give as much as they can. To the Red Cross, the Jewish and Christian foundations they all give no matter who it's for, from the Darfur regions of Africa, the tsunami victims in regions of the Far East, Pakistan earthquakes to our own New Orleans.

We give more than a lot of countries combined, yet to some receiving our aid, we are a true godsend. To others, they will still hate us just for who we are. We're a country born from immigrants from all over the world, all walks of life, who have come together, formed a nation, and became one under God; for we believe one nation under God with liberty and justice for all. Yes, it took us over two hundred years to achieve those words, yes, we're working on it. Still, America is not perfect. There's not a country that is. We welcome those of different faiths, cultures, hoping that they will blend in, for we have the freedom of religion, speech, and the press.

From the start, some said we would not last, so we elect our fellow citizens to office to pass and enact laws, to set an example for us all. It's a government that's ruled by its people. The people have the last word by going to the polls to show their support and then vote. There are some that come with intent to harm and to destroy. Others come for a better life, to leave the old one far behind.

Now our country is in great peril; it seems we're falling apart, splitting at the seams from Wall Street to the banks. From factories to our homes, it seems like we're losing it all. But look at the bright side. We've been there before, throughout our history from the start to Reconstruction, the Depression, to now. As bad as it seems, we still give to those who are in need. Now we must help each other from within, to get back on our own two feet.

We must throw out this greed, envy, and hate and come together once again. To rebuild this country, we must reopen our factories, rebuild our bridges, roads, and yes, our schools. We should have better health care for all and keep our jobs here, not abroad. We can do it. Yes, we can. Corporate America must stand up and take heed. One million in salary, that's all you get; that's all you need. No more bonuses, perks, stocks, and large retirement pay. No company jet, no penthouse suites, for if that's what you like, it comes out of your pay. Bring back reality from Wall Street to Main Street, from the Atlantic to the Pacific, from Alaska's north shores to the Gulf Coast. With faith in each other and from God above, we can do it, America. We've done it before.

WINTER INTO SPRING

As the warm days of spring that leads into summer, as the daffodils bloom and the brown grass of winter turn to green, as the robins and other birds start to make their nest, as we look out across this vast land of ours, we see nature at its very best. From the bright green leaves that shoot forth, from the giant oak trees, to the melting snow high up in the Rockies that form the streams that flow down to the rivers far below. To the deserts with the cactus in full bloom, to the fruit trees, the red buds, the dogwood, and more. All across this vast land, nature says it's time to be reborn. And all the beasts from small to large to the fowl give birth and raise their young. The land changes from dull brown to a carpet of living color, giving life where before it lay on the ground as no life at all.

And the same goes for its people, from sea to shiny sea. From the dead cold of winter, they wake up from a deep, cold freeze, awake to see our country in a mess. And some say there is no way to get out—companies going broke, homes being foreclosed, people being laid off from their jobs because of no work. But there is a bright side to this ordeal; there is a light that shines through all this, and it gets better as the people pull together as one, for as the winter that turns to spring, summer, fall, and to winter again, nature has a way to recycle itself to die and be reborn again.

So the people must start by looking at their own self from the inside out and remember those words he spoke of when he walked the earth, to do unto others as you would have them do unto you, for that is the golden rule. But to some, it does not matter whom they hurt. They have no pride, just a cold, cold heart. But we as a people, we can overcome by rebuilding and setting aside our differences and starting anew. Rebuild our economy from the ground up. From Wall Street to Main Street, from the Great Lakes to the Deep South, from Boston to LA, we can change this country, and there is just one way—we must trust in each other. And above all, we must trust in the one who created us; we must trust in God. For that light that shines so dim, it is us turning aside and letting our egos get the upper hand, and it's turning this country upside down. When we start trusting in each other and giving thanks to the one up above, that light will shine brighter and brighter and brighter still.

It will take a lot of effort from all sides. And then we can say, "Buy American, and buy it with pride." And then this country, even in the dead of winter, can still be alive and strong. For as nature, the seasons will still change from the harsh cold of winter to the rebirth of spring. America can stay in that spring all year long by rebuilding to make this country strong and shine with pride. And the people again will be reborn as the days of spring, and that light that once shined so dim will now burst into a rainbow of color. For it will mean our country has been reborn again.

TAKE A CHANCE

There comes a time in everyone's life when they must take a stand and choose what is right. The same goes for our country and our leaders as well. We must take the challenge, pull together all for one, one for all. Together we can make a difference. Oh yes, we can. But divided like Humpty Dumpty, we will have a great fall. So the challenges are here. They can be met if we take one step in the right direction—like a roll of dominoes, hit one and the rest most likely will fall. No jobs, millions being laid off, consumers can't spend, no factory output—there you have it, an economic downturn. People not working, they can't go out and spend. Then everything we have dreamed and worked for all goes down the drain, so we must, in some way, sit down and roll up our sleeves and figure a way out of this mess and put the people back to work. This stimulus package, will it worked? I don't know. We must wait and see. Build our factories here, not overseas; give them a credit for not going abroad. Make the interest rates come down, and on an even scale, lower the rates on homes. The banks will still make a lot.

They can make more by rolling back the executive pay and by giving the people a fair chance to get their jobs back and their homes at a lower rate. They will have more money to spend, and then we can say that by working together and believing in one another and the one about as we did in the past, we overcame then, and we can do it today if we have faith in each other and, above all, have faith in God.

NEW YORK, NEW YORK

He walks in that city that shows its buildings high up in the air, walking from Harlem all the way down to Times Square from the Bronx to the Upper East Side. He watches them, men, women, and their children talking to one another as the day goes by. Yes, the streets are filled with people going about their daily chores. And he smiles as the sun climbs higher and the shadows start to thin. What a beautiful day, not a cloud in the sky as he walks down the street on his merry way. He sees the churches, the synagogues, and the mosque where people go to meditate and to pray. From small shops to large ones all selling their wares to the restaurants that are on every street and their aroma that makes the mouth water and taste so sweet.

He smiles at the diversity from all walks of life, and he knows that out of all this, that man must make the choice to do right or do wrong. As he walks, he looks up and sees that statue that looks out into the sea. With her mighty arm raised and the torch that shines day and night, welcoming all who seek a much better life. From different countries and religions they do come, some with money, others just the clothes they wear. They have been coming for many a year, and when they see her standing so proud and tall, some will cheer, some will cry, but all in their own way will bow their heads and thank their God that they made it here at all.

With determination in their hearts and minds, they set out to forge a new life and leave the old one far behind. They started from nothing and built an empire far and wide from the Atlantic to the Pacific and everywhere in between. Some stayed in that city for generations, living in the same block. They say they wouldn't trade it for the world. Their heart and soul are embedded within; they made the city. The people from all walks of life, the city is like no other in this great nation of theirs from Wall Street to its Main Street and everywhere in between.

He looks at the city, its people both rich and poor. They must help each other; they must do more to help feed the hungry, clothe and shelter the poor. Do unto others as you would have them do unto you, for that is his golden rule. This could be any city, for he walks them all, but this is New York, and it's the largest of them all. He knows they are humans, and humans make mistakes, for they are not perfect by a long shot. When catastrophes hit, they look up to him and pray for guidance. And when they pray out or many, they become one in this city. There are millions of stories to be told. This is just one. He has walked this place from the beginning and will until the end. Things will happen, very good and very bad, and when they do, they will pray and ask why. Yes, there is evil all around, and it comes in many forms, spreading like cancer, entering man and eating at his very soul. And it's called many things, even greed, envy, and hate. So he looks out across this city he knows what will unfold.

Man must do the right thing. Help each other, set a goal, clean up the slums, rebuild the old and make new. You can do it; yes, you can. Look back to your forefathers; they did it by the sweat of their brow and the blood from their hands to make a better life for them back then and to their children and their children's children. Yes, New Yorkers, yes, you can.

PART THREE

OUR MILITARY

THE OLD VETERAN

A man standing on a knoll, looking down at the white stone slabs, all the same size, all perfectly lined up in a row. He bows his head, says a prayer, salutes, then sits down and begins to cry. He's a veteran, an old one at that, wearing his uniform that he has outgrown with all the metals pinned on his chest. As he cries, his mind wanders back to that time, that dreadful time when he knew he had to join to fight an enemy he didn't even know. All he knew was the world was at war; it was the honorable thing to do. At seventeen, barely a teen, he says good-bye to his family, praying to his God that he would see them again.

He went to Europe, fought in different campaigns, doing his job the best he knew how. He met a lot of friends from all walks of life, from the good old farm boys to the city slickers and others in between. He was a teen. He grew up fast and became a man. The first action he saw, he killed his first. Others told him he was the enemy, but in his heart he was someone's son, and he knew on the other side and also back home, moms were all the same, praying that their son would come back home alive. Doing the battles that he was in, he saw men on both sides being killed. It made him sick, and yet he went on. One campaign after another, a lot of his friends fell and gave their lives so that those back home could live in freedom. He heard stories of things that were so honorable, so honorable that no one would believe. This war he prayed how long must it go on.

Then the enemy retreated across the rhine. Then the bloodest of all battles begin and he was near the front lines.

A small bible he kept in his pocket next to his heart. Every day he would read it also to his comrades. Then some with him would kneel and pray. Then it happened early on a Friday morn. He got shot twice, once in the arm. The other bullet went in his chest; the bullet in the arm went all the way through. The one that hit his chest, by the grace of God, it hit his Bible then stopped. The bullet didn't go through; the Bible saved his life that day. He will never forget. It's in a case, the bullet, still intact in his living room on the mantel for all to see.

The battle, it raged on, and yes, we won. Then he was shipped to another place. The year 1945, he knew the war was almost over, and we were going to win. Then one morning he stood outside a large compound, the smell of death all around. As he entered, there were no guards. But what he saw, he could not believe his eyes. Buchenwald was the name of the camp. The prisoners were just skin and bones. He and his comrades carried them very, very gently outside, fed them, and he said with tears flowing down his cheeks, "You're going home." Then the war, it ended, and he returned home. He met some of those he carried in later years. They were living in New York, still with the numbers tattooed on their arm. They embraced, shared their stories.

Yes, it's hard to forgive. Now after the war, with a Bible in his hand, he preaches the Word of God. Every year he returns to pray for his comrades, their families, also the ones that he saved. Even the enemy, he leaves no one out. For he knows what the Bible says—"I forgive in a twinkle of an eye."

Then he gets up and looks at those stones one last time, for he knows it may be a year or two. Only God knows the day and hour he will return. Then he will join his comrades down there where those white stone slabs shine so brightly in the sun.

This story is dedicated to all veterans living and deceased, all the way back to our Revolutionary War of 1776.

THE SURVIVOR

A man old and bent with age sits at a window, watching the people go about their daily lives. He wonders how long it will be before he leaves this world and goes into that other world, the one that most of us believe. Then he looks at the numbers tattooed on his arm, faded, but yet can be seen. Tears come in his eyes as his mind wanders back to that time when he was a lad and not yet a teen.

He lived in a nice home on the outskirts of Berlin, his family not rich, middle class. His father worked at a bank six days a week. They were Jews but did not practice their faith. He was the youngest of the lot. The family got along with everyone and gave what they could to others. Whether they were Jews or Gentiles, it made no difference whom they were; his family gave what they could. He remembers his father saying, "We've been here for over three hundred years. Still they look down on us because of who we are."

Then the depression came. With everybody out of work, his father's job was cut back to three days a week. It was the same the world over. Back then, it took a while for the news to get around. Politics came into play, so they had to blame someone for what was going on. Then one man came to power. He could draw tens of thousands to hear him. They came from near and far. He had to blame someone, so he took it out on the Jews, saying they caused the depression. Then the man said. "They run our factories, our banks, our shops. They are the ones at fault. They're trying to take over. We must stop them at all costs."

Then it all started. All Jews had to wear a yellow star with papers just to get around. His father would say that things would be all right, that it would get better as time went by. The old man said, "Then it happened. We never believe it would. They came in the middle of the night, took us all away. I never saw my family again. They took them to a camp, I didn't know the name, but it was quite far away. I was fourteen, strong for my age. They forced me and others to work in factories making war machines. I was told to work hard, keep my mouth shut, do as I was told, and just maybe I could stay and not get shipped off to one of those camps. Those camps that no one ever comes back. Then we heard the news that Hitler—that's the man's name—invaded Austria. Then the war—that war, the war of all wars—began.

The only news we could get was what we overheard the guards would say. Then Germany invaded Poland, so England declared war. We were forced to work twenty hours a day. With very little to eat, my mind wandered. What happened to my cousins who left many years before to live in America, the land of the free, the home of the brave? They tried to get my father to go with them. He said Germany was his home, he wished them well, and he asked them to write—they did. But over the years, the letters just stopped coming. We were told all letters to Jews were read and then thrown away. To the outside world, we were dead.

Then we heard the news. We cheered and cried to ourselves. America had entered the war, and we believed it would end overnight. Then one day, all new people, Germans, all of them replaced us. We were taken away. They loaded us on boxcars, sent us to a place called Buchenwald. We were told we would never get out of that place alive. We were not humans, just skin on bones. The year was 1944 when we arrived. we were separated from the others. Me and a few that were stronger did the work; the work I cannot speak of or describe even to this day. This went on day and night. We had very little to eat, cabbage or turnip soup if we were lucky, and our determination to stay alive. After years, most of us were so weak that we could not get up off the wooden bunks. By morning, some beside us, the lucky ones, they would already be dead. Then one morning when we awoke, there were no guards and it was very, very quiet. Then we heard tanks, trucks, words we could not understand. The doors swung open, and a man in uniform, different from those of the guards, entered. His eyes and his mouth were open. As he looked around, he started to cry. He spoke English. "He's American," we cried. Then he said, "You're free." And he and other soldiers picked us up and carried us outside.

Now many, many years have passed. We told the world what happened. Still a lot do not believe. All my family's gone now, just memories of what used to be. I never got married, afraid of what might happen, I guess. I'm now an American. I tell people, both Jews and Christians and others if they wish to hear, what happened, what I did. I told them the stories of my childhood, what little that I had. I see into their eyes, the tears running down their cheeks. I tell them we should remember, never forget, for it could happen again like Germany, lest we forget, even after all these years. I still wake up in the middle of the night to that smell, the taste. It's still on my mind, so I will never forget. I'm now old and well past my prime, just sitting and waiting for that time. And when it comes, that angel, some say the angel of death, I pray he carries me away to a much better and safer place. In that place we all, no matter who we are, can hold hands and live in peace in God's kingdom. All of us, for that's where I want to be.

This story is dedicated to my closest friend Louis Bosyk, whose family died at Auschwitz because of who they were, and also to millions of other Jews.

And to the Christians who helped, also to the gays and others just because of who or what they were.

To all of you, rest in peace.

Your revenge will be at the end of time.

THE HERO

A man and a woman all dressed in black are waiting at the station for the train to arrive. As the train pulls in, they squeeze each other's hand. Then the train stops. Nine men all dressed in uniform disembark, carrying a flag-draped casket. Then they stop in front of the man and woman. One steps forward, salutes, and says, "Mr. and Mrs. James, your country thanks you for the sacrifice that your son has made. He's a hero. We leave no man behind, and we with your blessings will bury our comrade, your son, with the highest of honors. He gave his life for his fellow man and his country. Private First Class James was our friend." Then he salutes, turns, and they carried James to a hearse then to the home, then later to church where services will be held, and finally to the family plot where James will be laid to rest.

James's pallbearers were his comrades-in-arms. He saved all of them. Yes, he gave his life so they could live. They told his parents what happened. He was a medic, hoping after his tour that he would go back to school, then college, then return home as a doctor. That's what he wanted, but as in life, sometimes it doesn't happen that way. He enlisted to serve his country and to go to school. After basic, he went to study medicine, so he became a medic. It was easy for him. He studied hard. Learning all that he could for the short time he had, he then got his orders. Packed his bags. Then off to Iraq.

As a medic, he treated a lot. Some of those he treated had minor injuries while others that he treated didn't make it to base at all. But he gave all he had, praying he could give more. Before he left, his dad gave him a small Bible to keep in his shirt with pages marked. It was his grandfather's Bible he had during World War II. He would read it, and it was still in good shape. As he would read it, some of his comrades would join in, a song or a prayer, for they all knew this might be the last day of their life. They were tight-knit. They told each other about their families, where they came from, what they wanted to do after their tour. They knew what James wanted at base. He would read upon the latest in medicine, how to do this and that, more than what he was taught.

It was a nightmare for all, the roadside bombings or the bombings in the marketplace, where many would be killed, the children left lame or homeless with no parents. It was hard for James. He had three sisters and a brother back home. It would be hard even for them. Then on a Tuesday, their patrol set out around 10:00 a.m. It was just starting to get hot. As they entered a village, they were told to be extra careful. Reports about the movement of al-Qaeda were around. Halfway through, everything seemed fine.

Then the shooting started from rooftops and from the rear, then from the front. They were surrounded from all sides. They took cover with what little they had. Then three of his comrades got hit and were lying out in the street. He went running, pulling them all to safety under heavy fire. They called in for support. Then as he was patching up his comrades the best he could, two more got hit. Under heavy fire, he ran as fast as he could and pulled them to safety. They were hit, but the bullets went clear through.

Then two kids no older than five who were hiding in a doorway ran across the street. Then someone on the roof opened fire, and the boy was hit. James went running, grabbed the boy, and he was shot in the leg. The girl kept running as James got the boy. James got shot three times but carried him to safety, went back for the girl with no concern for himself, and he staggered with the girl. By then reinforcements arrived and killed all the insurgents. They took all the wounded back to base, even the boy and girl. All the men that were hit made it OK. James saved them all that day. For James, the doctors could do no more; he knew he was going to die. He called his comrades to be by his side and told them, "I did this for you, those kids, the freedom they all hunger for. Tell my mom and dad I'll miss them. I will wait for them on the other side." Then his comrades touched him for the last time. They saw a smile on his face. He pointed, saying, "Do you see the light? Do you see the light? It's calling my name. I'm now going home."

James was given full military honors, with his comrades by his side.

It was cloudy that day, ready to pour down rain. Then they folded the flag and presented it to his mom as the taps sounded with the twenty-one-gun salute. A miracle happened—the clouds parted as if drawing back the blinds, and a bright ray of light came and settled directly on James's casket. They all smiled, for now they all knew James was home with his real Father in that place that's across the bridge in paradise.

THE VETERANS

Veterans are a group of people from all walks of life, men and women from different religions, race, and ethnic backgrounds. These men and women, they serve to protect their loved ones back home. Most now are volunteers; the last draft was Vietnam. We pray we don't see the draft again. The vets, they serve, serve their country with pride. A lot of them, they leave their husbands, wives, and kids to join for different reasons. Some because of the economics, others to improve and enrich their lives, but they are vets, war vets or peacetime.

When you see a veteran or one in uniform, shake his hand, salute, show him you care. To those that lost their lives in Iraq, Afghanistan, back to Vietnam, even to our revolution, we must never forget them and the reason they gave the ultimate price. Today a lot of vets are being neglected from health care down to losing their homes. It seems as though some people just don't care. We are a vast country, the greatest the world has ever seen. Our vets served with pride. Let's show them the same, for without them where would this country be? Stop and think about it. You will agree.

They are the backbone of this country. They will protect it down to the last man. So if a vet is losing his home because of high installment rates and if foreclosure is on the way, a little help in refinancing will get him on his way. Then we should do it. To those retired vets, I do understand, for I am with you; I'm a vet. Retired, on a fix income. So let's come together, vet and nonvet alike. Help each other turn this country around, and when that time comes, when we put the vet to rest, give them the honor they deserve. Then God in his mercy will receive them in that place. That place on the other side that's called paradise.

I'M A VET

I remember that day when I held my mother close with tears in my eyes. Saying good-bye was the hardest thing I had to do. When the driver said it was time to leave and I had to get on board, it was hard for me to do. Uncle Sam was calling. Leaving Mom on the farm alone as I pulled away from her, she said, "You be good and do as they say and come back home safely to me someday."

Fort Knox was calling, and it was cold and damp, eight weeks of training before sunup and after sundown. I'm from the hills, but misery and some others—those hills as you look up. And say where's the top and where do they end? But by sweat and tears, I made it through and on to Benning and another eight weeks still. Going there were three buses strong, full of soldiers, and I was in charge. Crossing at that time was the Mason and Dixon line—all the black soldiers had to get up and sit in the back, and they had to eat in an area far away from the whites. And I hated it, but protesting did no good. Segregation, that's what it's called, even in uniform of their country, to the South they were still black. At Benning it was better than Knox. No high mountains to climb with full field pack. Then came those men in high spit-shined boots, asking for volunteers to join them for adventure that would last three full years or to some a life time. So a few of us said yes.

So to Fort Bragg, I went to join the airborne and jump out of planes. You got to be kidding. Am I insane? But extra pay, yes, that sealed the deal. It was worse than Knox and Benning combined, and then came that day when I first jumped and left the plane and floated to the ground, shaking the sand from my boots, I smiled and said, "Now that was fun." Then on leave I told Mom what I did, and she said, "Now I know you're insane." And I told her, "But, Mom, I like it. It's hard work, but at the same time, it's fun."

Then overseas to Okinawa, I went, joining the rock, named for the men who jumped in the Philippines. You know that war, World War II. After many jumps going here and there, I look back, and now I call myself a veteran. I was proud to serve so others could be free. I prayed to God, and I made it home to Mom. Her prayer came true. To those who lost their lives for a cause in which they believe, to their families, yes, they gave all. To the veterans that's up in their years. (For you and me.) Yes, we're a country. We must take care of them year after year. They served, they fought, and they did their best.

We fought as volunteers to set our country free. To the present day, men and women in uniform, they deserve our help every minute of the day. So fly the flag and give them a cheer, for without them, we might not be here free and safe. Now the military and all the rest from North, East, West, and the South, now we can say we're of one race—the human race. For he created you and me in his image. To the veterans now and then, stand tall and proud and don't give in. For old glory, its stars and stripes, still it waves high. So to our veterans who gave it all, I say Godspeed and God bless us all.

JIM AND NAM

This story is true—I will not name names or places. I was hired to work in a small plant with about thirty-five workers building panels for a large company. I was one of the oldest, yet not that old. I had at least seven workers higher up in seniority than me. I made it to work on time, never late, and I did my job. After a few months, I was asked by some workers if I would represent them as a union or shop steward. We belong to a union but had no rep. At that time, I was thirty-five; most were under twenty-five.

Within a few months, I got everybody a raise. Within a year, the shop had grown into another line. I was offered the job as general foreman overall, with extra pay. I accepted, gave up my union, then on a Friday the plant manager told me that if everything was finished and cleaned up, he would have beer for all. Only two said no to beer, they didn't drink. I informed them, and we had beer and started talking about one thing to another. I didn't know how it started, but religion was brought up. Two were Mormons, two Baptists, and so on. One man, I'll call him Jim, looked at me. "What are you?" he asked. "My parents were Baptist. I'm a holiness from Southern Ohio. "What are you?" He looked at me, and I said, "I don't believe in God. I'm an atheist."

"Jim, you don't believe in God?"

"No, I don't. No one can prove it."

"No, no one can. It's faith."

Then someone asked Jim, "Jim, didn't you tell me you served in Vietnam?"

"Yeah."

"Jim, you were in Nam during the conflict?"

"Yeah."

"Weren't you there?"

"No, I was stationed on Okinawa. We had a few officers from Nam training with us. I didn't see any action.

"What was your job there?"

"I was a machine gunner."

"So you saw a lot of action?"

"Sure."

"Jim, do you know if you killed any Vietcongs?"

"Guess I did. They were dead, or the men in my squad did."

"Let me ask you a question. Would you tell me the truth?"

"Ask away."

"Was there at one point during your tour over there that you saw action so bad you didn't know if you were going to live or die?"

"Sure, a number of times."

"Think back if you would to the worst time, tell us about it."

"Well, we were on patrol. We would find tunnels, blow them up. We had been out for some time. We were all tired, with hardly any sleep, on our way back in. Bango shots were fired. We hit the ground. Before you knew it all hell broke loose. The Vietcong were shooting from all sides. They had us pinned down. We had nowhere to retreat, several of the men were hit. We called in choppers, they were the ones that saved us that day. We all got out alive. A few were hit, but none died."

"I'm glad, Jim. There is one question I'd like to ask you. If those choppers didn't come when they did, what would have happened?"

"Hell, we all would be dead."

"OK, let's say how long did you have between the call and the choppers' arrival?"

"Just minutes."

"So with a couple of minutes, you all would have been dead."

"Yep."

"Here's the question. During those minutes, you knew you were going to die if those choppers didn't show up. Am I right?"

"Yeah, you're right."

"Then why, Jim, why did you pray?"

During the entire time, no one spoke except Jim and me.

Jim didn't answer. He finished his beer, got up, and left. No one said anything. After a few minutes, we cleaned up. I closed and locked up.

A week went by. No one said anything about what happened. Then one afternoon, Jim called me to one side. He said, "You got me back there when we were talking about Nam and God."

"Well, Jim, you still haven't given me an answer. Why did you pray?"

I could see a tear in his eye.

"Yeah, I prayed. I didn't want to die. God saved us all that day."

"Then why are you going against him now. Jim? When it comes to a minute or two, you don't know if you're going to live or die. You're going to pray. It doesn't matter who you are."

"Guess you're right. No, I know you're right. After you asked that question, I started to think I do believe.

"Jim, you don't have to pin it on your shirt. If someone asks, smile and say yes, don't you?"

Jim still drank and rode a motorcycle. I pray he made it OK and got right with God. Within a month, he was killed riding his cycle without a helmet while he was driving over the limit. We all went to his service, and as I looked at him, I prayed Jim was on the other side. What I said back there about praying, I prayed Jim was all dressed up with somewhere to go.

This is true. It happened many years ago. I pray that Jim is with his Maker across the bridge on the other side in paradise.

PART FOUR

STORIES FOR ALL TO READ

GRANDPA, HOW OLD DID YOU SAY YOU ARE?

We have heard stories some we wish were true, but some stories, some have good endings, some not. Some endings could go either way. Here is one such story I hope you enjoy.

A young man arrived in a small town. It was small, yet it had a nice atmosphere about it. He smiled to himself as he looked around, thinking it looked almost the same as it did years back as he walked down the street to American Diner, the only diner in town. He looked in the window of a vacant building. Seeing his reflection, he said, "You still look the same after all these years." As he entered, a middle-aged woman said hello and showed him a seat. He asked for coffee and the menu. Then she brought the coffee and gave him the daily paper to read. A small paper no more than ten pages. All old news. The paper was only printed twice a month. Within a few minutes, a young teen, no older than sixteen, came out and set his breakfast down. Instead of leaving, the teen stared at the customer with big round eyes and a wide-open mouth.

"Is anything wrong, young man?"

"No, sir, I thought we had met before."

"I don't think so. It's my first time in town."

"I'm sorry, please enjoy your meal."

The teen left and went behind the counter. Within a few minutes, he took off on his bike and headed for home. He was so excited that he dropped his bike, ran up the steps onto the porch, then stopped dead in his tracks. There sitting in the rocker was his seventy-five-year-old great-grandmother, but her age or looks was not of a seventy-five-year-old. She looked much younger. Also, her mind was that of a younger person.

"Hi, Gramps."

"Hi, Billy. What are you doing home? You're supposed to be at the diner, helping your mom and dad."

"Oh, they know I'm here. I have to go and get something. I'll be right back."

As he entered the house, he went directly to Gramps's room, took down a picture of Gramps taken on her wedding day alone with her husband. She was a beautiful woman back then. He smiled. She still is. Then he looked at her husband, his great-grandfather. The man at the diner was the spitting image of his great-grandfather. But how could this be? He knew the family history on both sides better than anyone else other than Gramps. He kept every detail written down. It would make a great book one day, so how could this be? She was twenty-three; he was twenty-five when they got married. That was many, many years back, 1923 to be precise. Just a coincidence until he saw that scar over his right eye on his forehead. Then he remembered a picture he had of him. His name was George Preston. He renamed the diner American Diner.

Everyone said he would grow up and look just like him minus the scar. He then goes out and talks to Gramps.

"Gramps, I know it's none of my business, may I ask you something?"

"Billy, ask all you want."

"Go back, way back, before you were married. Tell me about him, your husband, my great-grandfather. When you met, everything, leave nothing out."

"Why, Billy?"

"Oh. Sorry. Summer assignment. We have to write about someone or make up someone for a term. You never talk about him, so I thought it would make a good story, a mystery so to speak."

"Well, I don't talk about it much, brings back good times, bad times. If I tell you, you will think I'm nuts."

"No, Gramps, to me it will be your story. If you say it's the truth, it's the truth. At school it will be just another story."

"Very well. As you know, our family has been in this town from day one. We're the oldest. We started this town in 1800. As far as I know, we came from England, the Manchester area. His new bride was from Scotland. From what I was told, they met while he was working on a farm. They fell in love, married. Both back then had a little saved up. They were not servants. They were hired help, so they got better pay. They saved and came to America. They settled here to farm. Got one of those land grants. He was good at farming and had some knowledge of building barns. So that's the way it started. From what was told to me, it was hard for them the first few years, then other people moved in the same area, so in later years he built and opened a store with a few rooms to let like an inn. Then it was called a trading post. The diner was the trading post, oldest building in town. Over the years, they had four children, one boy, three girls. The girls got married, moved away across the Mississippi. Never heard from them again. The boy became the head of the household after his father died. A few years later, his mom died. You know the story. They're buried in the family plot at Old Groves cemetery. You mow it every month.

"One day, after I'm gone, you had better trim my grave with care and plant a yellow rose bush to remind you of me when you get my age. Thomas worked the farm, but it was hard to do both, so he put word out for someone to run the inn. Soon his message was answered. He hired a woman and her young daughter to run the inn while he worked the farm. Then one thing led to another. They fell in love and were married, and it continued until I was born in 1900. In 1920, that's when I first saw him. He came to the diner over the years. The diner had changed from an inn to a diner, the same but yet different. I was helping Mom and Dad. He was the most handsome man I ever seen. He got a job at the local mill. He knew more about running a mill than the owner did. Guess to both of us it was love at first sight. Even Mom and Dad knew. Said he was from the Philadelphia area. He had no living kin, just said he was looking for a place to settle down, that's what he wanted. Yet something was holding him back.

"Then in 1923, before the Depression, we were married and had one son, your grandfather. As time went by, he still worked at the mill. During those times, we all lived together. Then the mill closed, so he started working at the diner. It was hard, those Depression years. He was different. He gave a lot of food away, but we still managed to get by. Then the war started. Your grandfather was called up. Because of the war and people working for the war effort, things improved. When your grandfather returned, it was a great reunion. Bill worked at the diner just like before the war. When he returned, he brought back lots of recipes from Italy—all kinds of pasta dishes and, yes, pizza. I was forty-six then. Yes, looking my age, but George hadn't aged one day. Not one day, no hair loss, no gray, same as the day I first saw him.

"Bill asked me about it. All I could say, it must be in his blood. Now it's called genes. I told Bill it might pass on to you. A few months later, I saw George in the bedroom with no clothes on, butt naked. Looking at himself in the mirror all over, he didn't see me, but tears were running down his face. I never asked, but maybe I should have. Within a month, he went to open the diner. He never made it there. It was as if the ground had swallowed him up. He disappeared. Later, I found a letter under his pillow, addressed to me. It told me his life story, the life before we met. I still have the letter, knowing that one day before I die, he will return to say good-bye. I believe what he said in the letter. It's sealed, and when I die, it will be given to you. Billy, you have seen his picture. If you had his scar on your forehead, you would pass for his twin. Your grandfather loved him so much. I wanted to tell but was asked not to. It broke my heart when your grandfather, my son, died, but I keep my word, it's my bond. Your grandfather married then your father was born. Later, like his father, he got married.

"Billy, I would give you the letter now. But I keep my word. One day, you will know, then it's up to you to believe or not."

"Gramps, are you saying he's still alive and looks the same as the day you and him got married?"

All Gramps did was smile with tears in her eyes. As Billy leaned over and kissed Gramps, he left to go back to the diner, entering the back door. Very few people were there. The man was still there, reading the paper, so Billy did his work like every day. Out of the corner of his eye, he watched the man until he got up, paid his bill, looked around at the place, and told his mom, "Good meal. Looks like this place has been here for a long time."

"The diner has been in this family since it was built for way over a hundred years, a trading post before that.

"So this is your diner?"

"Yes, I married into it. And after we're gone, we hope it will be in our son's hands. That's him, Billy, over there."

When he looked, they both knew. As Billy opened the door, he saw a tear in the man's eye. Then he knew this was George Preston, his great-grandfather. But what should he do? After the man left, he asked his mom to be excused. He would come back after choosing to clean up. Before she could answer, he ran out the back door and got on his bike. He knew where George was going. He could cut across the park and be back home before George could get there. Within minutes, a car pulled up. George parked it on the other side of the road away from the house, got out, and stood behind some pines as Billy watched. Tears were flowing down the man's face as he looked at Gramps sitting on the porch. Teens sometimes do things before they think, and Billy was no different.

"What are you doing?"

The man froze as Billy came up to him. As they looked at each other, Billy said, "I know you, I know who you are. Be a man. Go to your wife. That's if you're not afraid."

The man with tears flowing down his face looked at Billy. "How did you know?"

"Look at me. Put a scar on my forehead. I would be a dead ringer in a couple of years, just like you, your twin. Instead, you're my great-grandfather. How can this be?"

As George wiped the tears from his eyes, he looked at Billy, who walked up to him, and said, "Do you have a lifetime? If so, I'll tell you, but no one else would believe. No one but your wife, I just talked to her. She still has your letter. After she's gone, the letter will be given to me. She told me you would come back to her. One last time, tell her why you went away before she dies. So tell me, then her. Let's sit down, for this will take some time."

As George stared at his great-grandson and across the way at his wife, he said, "What I'm about to tell you is the truth. It's the story of my life. I won't go through all the details, just the ones you should know. I'm not an evil person. Truth is, I'm a man of God just like you. Things happen that no one can explain. If everyone knew about me, I would be in a lab, poked on like a rat. Please, son, what I'm about to tell you is the truth. Please don't butt in until I'm finished.

"Yes, my name is George Preston. I was born to a working-class family on the outskirts of Philadelphia on August the first, the year 1760. My father worked at a mill, my mother worked as a maid. We lived on the owner's property. He also owned the mill. Dad was good at his job, the best I've seen. He came here from England in 1742. They had four other children. They all died of fever before the age of five. Then I was born. I was lucky I never had a sick day in my life. When I got older, I worked with my dad at the mill. The smell of the flour and the grain, guess it stayed with me. Even now I can smell the aroma. It smells so sweet. I'm going to make this short. The whole story will take your lifetime. When we declared independence from England and the war started, I was all eager to join. I had never shot a gun before.

"We lived in the city or the edge. The owner of the mill and Dad also wanted independence, so I joined like so many other men, young and old. Dad also wanted to join. But the owner said we could do more here sending meal and grain to the troops, so that's the way it was. No basic training as long as you could see. Loaded the chambered, and aimed a gun, you were in. In September of '76, I was sixteen. We were in a battle in the upper part of Pennsylvania. Fighting lasted all day. Hit, run, and miss, like hide-and-seek. Then by all accounts, I slipped and went down a large embankment. I was knocked out. How long? When I woke up, it was sunset. Where the rest of the men went, I didn't know. Guess they thought I was dead. That's where the scar came from. Once I could stand, I started climbing the embankment or hill. That's when I saw my gun was busted. It hit a rock and split. The barrel was bent a little, and near the summit a red coat saw me. I was so close, all I could see was the devil in his eyes. He gave off one shot, and he hit me there, see that star at the edge of the scar? My hair covers it up. That's where the bullet went in. Guess it's still there. It healed over in time.

"I fell over a hundred feet facedown in a creek bed. The red coat didn't come down to see if I was dead. I didn't move, falling a hundred feet. He went on. When I woke up, the sun was overhead, it was noon. I tried to stand, but I was too weak, so I stayed hidden on the bank for almost two days. Going in and out of consciousness, finally

I started walking up the creek, hoping to find the other members of the company and hoping that they were headed up the same way. At about sundown, I heard voices and recognized them. They came running. They fed and kept me warm. There was nothing more they could do. The next day, we met up with a larger company, and they dropped me off on a farm.

"Within a week, I was back home. A doctor checked me out and said the bullet was too deep in my forehead. He was afraid to operate because it may cause more damage, so if it hasn't dissolved it's still there. The fighting stopped, and my head healed except for the scar. A few years passed. That's when I noticed my parents and friends were getting older while I was still the same. Maybe it was the bullet, I don't know. Then everybody started talking. I told my parents I had to leave and why. They understood. As time went by, I saw them as often as I could. Before they died, they said to seek God's advice, he would know what to do. I asked God, maybe this was my destiny, for almost two hundred years from the time I left home, I went from town to town no more than a few years at each place. I met a lot of nice people. One thing I never did, I never married. I was afraid.

"That is, until I met your gramps. I fell head over heels in love. Until that time, I was with no other. I should have said no and kept on going. Have you ever said no to Gramps? Instead I married her, afraid at first. Then I prayed again and hoped maybe I would start to age. It never happened. Then rumors started like before. It broke my heart when I left, so I wrote her that letter and told her how it all started. I left nothing out. You and the rest of the family never knew I was at everyone's funeral. Now when someone dies, it's in the paper, so every few years I would slip back at first from afar. Then about twenty years back on our anniversary, no one was at home, just her. I got up the nerve and walked up those steps. She was in the rocker just like now. She just smiled and held out her arms and said, 'I knew you would be back.'

"She told me after she saw me in front of the mirror, then reading the letter, that she knew everything was true. We made a promise not to tell no one, not even you. Gramps, she keeps her word, so sometimes I look at her from here when I know no one's around. I go to her, tell her what I've done, her the same. I'm over two hundred years old now. I don't want to go through any more of this. It's time I lay my body down next to my true love when it's time."

"Look, Gramps is now seventy-five years old. You still look around twenty-five, give or take a year. Mom and Dad, if Gramps would tell them, and because we all love her so much, they would believe and welcome you with open arms. No one else would have to know. You can stay here with us or above the diner. It's up to you and Gramps. I'll abide by what she says. Oh yeah, you could be our distant cousin from one of the girls that married and moved across the Mississippi. So look, I don't know what to call you, so I'll call you George when we're around people. Alone or with family, it will be Grandpa. So, Grandpa, what do you say you and me go together up those stairs, the three of us will discuss it. As I said, I will abide by what you two decide."

Then they both got up. George looked across the way at Gramps then at Billy. When their eyes met, tears in each, they embraced. George, now Grandpa, hugged Billy so hard that Billy almost passed out. Then looking at Billy, he said, "I've never hugged anyone, not since my son, your grandfather, died. I knew he loved me so much. See, I would come back over time, see him and Gramps from afar. I made a mistake back then. I should not have left. When he died, the night before the funeral, I slipped into the home. Back then it was not locked. I spent over two hours with him. I then picked him up and held him for I don't know how long. Afterwards, I put two roses in his hand, one yellow, the other white. The next day, Gramps picked up the roses at his grave. I saw her look around. I then knew that she knew I was still around. She put them in a case, brown but still intact. Billy, is this what you want?"

"Yes, I'll write a book one day about all this. It will be the best—fiction of course, book of the year. Names would have to be changed to protect you know who."

"Very well, then, let's go and hope she doesn't have a heart attack when she sees us."

When they started around the side yard, Grandpa put his arms around Billy. Halfway across, Gramps saw them. She got up and almost fell down the steps. And the two went running to help her to her feet. As they stared at each other then embraced, no one said a word. Then Gramps looked at Billy. "Is this why you asked about me and George?"

"Yes, Gramps. He came in the diner. When I put the plate down, I saw the scar. I just knew who he was. I came running. And the way you told it, you were not mad. Most women would be furious, so I followed him. I knew he would be coming here."

They talked. The three talked and made a decision. It was almost seven when Billy's parents got home. He met them on the porch. His dad, a tall, lean man, just looked at him and asked, "And where have you been all day?"

"Dad, Mom, please sat down. What I'm about to tell you, it will blow your mind."

The lights in the house were on all night. The next morning, all five were around the kitchen table. George, now Grandpa, after they sat down, said a prayer. But he could not finish as he was choked up. Billy, who has prayed but only to himself, took over, asking God to mend the family. It would be left up to him what the outcome would be, so that's how it was. Grandpa worked at the diner as a distant cousin and lived upstairs but was at the family home most of the time. Billy also worked at the diner and still mowed the cemetery. The family plot was very large.

One day, he prayed that many years from now he would be laid to rest next to Gramps, his parents and he hoped his grandpa. As the years passed, Billy went to state and majored in—what else—American history. He was a wiz. He had a master's degree as a teacher, also in literature. He still lived in the family home, got a teaching job at state and had written a best-selling fiction book, of course titled *Grandpa, How Old Did You Say You Are?*

Gramps and Grandpa shared the remaining years together. Then at the age of eighty-five, Gramps passed away. Before she died, she told her love, "I had a dream. I saw gray in your hair. You started to age. In my dream, God answered our prayer, there is a mystery to God." Grandpa's hair started to turn gray little by little as she was dying. Grandpa told her he had a feeling he would follow her real soon. They planted a yellow rose bush on Gramps's grave.

Then, Grandpa, in a few years at breakfast, started bleeding from his forehead. By nightfall, a very small piece of lead came out. It was encrusted. He picked it up and said, "I saw this in my dream. I saw you, Billy, burying me next to Gramps. I believe God has answered my prayer."

Within six months, Grandpa called his family to his side. "It's time. I have lived a long life, I wish it on no man." Then he smiled. "I knew someday I would see the light. It's calling my name."

Grandpa was buried next to his true love. On the marker was written "Born August 1, 1760, died September 5, 1991." If anyone asked the answer was that they just put the wrong year on and that they'll be around to change it someday.

Billy smiled. And yes, he still mows the cemetery and trims two rose bushes, one yellow, the other white.

When finished, he sat on a stone seat and looked at his entire family, with tears in his eyes and a smile on his face. He knows one day, maybe tomorrow or many years down the road, he will join his family like his grandpa, smiling as he goes into the light.

A lot of stories end here. As time went by, Billy looked in the mirror. Something was different. A red mark had appeared above his eye on his forehead. It looked like it was taking shape. Yes, like a scar. So he finished shaving, got dressed, and checked out of the diner. He still owned it. Mom and Dad took an early retirement. He hired a few to work it the same way as before, and then he was off to school.

Once in a while, he reaches up and scratches his forehead. So then he wondered about that saying, "What goes around, comes around." Then without thinking, he stopped the car. He looked again in the rearview mirror and looked at the red mark. Did Grandpa's genes caused what has happened to him. Now has passed it onto him, nah?

RAMOS AND PEREZ

This story is about a gang leader and a young rookie cop. This could happen in any city. Gangs, no matter who they are or where they're at, they destroy families, neighborhoods, and sometimes entire cities. Ramos is one. Even the leader won't cross him. He does things with the gang and also on his own. Some say his eyes turn red, then black, as if the devil himself were inside of him. He's been in trouble from what his parents say from the time he was born. At seven, he was taken from his home and placed by the courts in juvenile detention for beating up and nearly killing a six-year-old, all over a pack of gum. The judge said, "You young man, you have no remorse." All Ramos did was just stare at the judge with hate in his eyes.

Even in detention, everyone backed away. Two other boys, three years older than Ramos, decided enough was enough. They got him alone, but Ramos was stronger than most boys his age. When it was over, the two boys were beaten so bad, they had to be taken to the ER. Ramos was put under heavy supervision until he reached eightteen then the court released him. The same judge said, "I don't want to see you in here again." Without a word, he left. He didn't even glance at his parents. Within a month, he robbed a small carryout and told the clerk, "If you tell, I'll be back and put a bullet in your head." As word got out, he joined a gang. The leader, Che, started to tell him the rules, but backed away after looking in his eyes.

Besides having a cold heart, Ramos was smart. Even in detention he failed every subject, but inside he knew every word. He had a photographic memory. He kept it to himself. The gang started to grow and spread out. To do business in their turf, you had to pay up. Then one afternoon, a few members of another gang ended up on the wrong side of town. Shooting broke out. When it was over, five gang members were dead from the rival gang. Three, including Che, from the south side were dead. Nobody saw anything. The police knew everyone was afraid. One word to the police, even by phone, you or a member of your family would probably end up dead.

So Ramos took over; they all voted and all said yes. They put Che and the other two to rest. Afterward, Ramos alone went to the north side, took revenge, and then the word got out. If you saw Ramos or any member of his gang, you went to the other side of the street. As time went by, Ramos had a reputation to uphold; no one could do him harm. Now at age twenty-three, his rap sheet was a mile long. But as fate had it, no one would come forward, so he walked away. Charges after charges were dropped, and no one would go to the south end. Even the police had two cars no more than a minute of each other.

Then a new recruit class got their badges. Now twenty more cops were on the street. One rookie named Perez knew all about the gangs. His two older brothers were killed in a gang fight when he was only two. His mother was now single, and his father died of an overdose when he was only one. His older brothers were fourteen and sixteen when they were killed, so in the middle of the night, his mom packed their bags and moved out. She wanted more for her son and herself. With the help of the church, they got her a job in another city. When Perez got old enough, she told him everything and left nothing out. Afterward, Perez held his mother close, saying, "You did the right thing. I will make you proud of me someday." So the day he got his badge, his mother all in tears, saying, "I am so proud of you. You will make rookie of the year."

Even after she told him about his father and two brothers, Perez studied hard and went to all the meetings the police would have. He learned about the gangs, so by the time he got out of school, he was a wiz. So he enrolled in the police academy in his hometown. At first his mother said no. He smiled and said, "Mom, you changed our name, and it's been twenty years. Besides, we're not living in the south end or north end. We're living downtown. You will be safe. You will have me by your side."

Now Perez was twenty-two and patrolling the south end with his partner, Harris, a thirty-five-year-old patrolman for ten years. After a couple of weeks, Harris looked at Perez, and said, "You know a lot about gangs, the south—and north-enders more than what they teach at the academy."

"Look, Bob—sorry, Sergeant Harris, don't tell anyone, not even the captain what I'm about to tell you."

So Perez told Harris all he knew and how he knew it. "So you're a southsider. I was two when I left with my mom. I wanted to make my mom proud of me."

"Well, I think you have made her proud now. But Ramos is one dude we have to watch out for. He's smart and has been in and out of jail. We can only keep him for a few days. He's smart enough not to leave anything at the scene."

"Mom was here when that Che was running things. She doesn't know anything about this Ramos guy. Well, one thing we do know but can't put two and two together is that Ramos, about three years ago, killed a store owner and his son for not paying protection. They moved in and opened a carryout. That's when Ramos's men paid them a visit. The father and son were from Egypt. Said no, this was America, the police were their protectors. Their name was Syad, and they called the police. We watch out for them. Only one member would go in, buy something, and bring up the protection again, then leave. We never could catch Ramos. Then around midnight, when the Syads were closing, that's when they were both shot in the head. That's Ramos's style. No one heard or saw nothing until a patrol car saw the lights were still on. When they went in, well, you know the rest. The case is still open, not a single clue. We know Ramos did it, proving it is another thing."

For the next few weeks, Perez and Harris got to know each other and the south end. They paid a visit to the same carryout. It had been closed for almost three years. Now another couple with two kids has opened the store. They knew what happened, and they thought things would be different. They didn't sell liquor or any alcoholic beverage; their Christian faith forbid drinking, but they seemed like nice people.

"I've seen them hand out food to some of the street people. They are making an impression on the area and are well liked. What about Ramos, has he or his men been around? According to the Hills, they told them to pay up. They said no. So far, nothing has happened. Do you think Ramos will let them by?"

"Heck no. He'll give them time. Then he will go and see them if we're not around God help them. Ramos, after taking over the gang, had many run-ins with the law."

Like Harris said, he was street-smart, but these people, the Hills, they didn't sell alcohol. All the people in the area liked them for that. But it was ruining his enterprise, so it was time to pay them a visit. Ramos smiled. He had already killed two in the same building three years back. If they didn't comply and start paying their dues, just maybe the same would happen to them. He had to go early, for they closed at nine. Most of the stores that sold beer, they stayed open at least till midnight or later. He knew what the Hills looked like. They have never seen him, so it should be a piece of cake.

Ramos left the gang and started out on his own. No one had ever seen him kill anyone. He wanted it that way. Then if anything would happen, no one could snitch, for no one had seen anything.

About eight thirty, the Hills were cleaning up. Mr. Hill looked at his wife and teenage son, and said, "Hope we don't have to use this." He pointing to a button near the register. It was a silent alarm. Mr. Hill said, "Patrolman Harris showed us the photo of Ramos. If he comes in, one of us stand here and have your finger on the button. We had five put in all over the store. Only we know where they are at."

"Dad, do you think Ramos will make good at what his men said?"

"Yes, I do, but we have to take a stand. God will take care of us, he's never let us down."

Then at about closing time, Ramos stepped inside and introduced himself. "Have you made up your mind? Are you going to pay or not?"

"No, we're not paying."

Then Ramos pulled out his gun and pointed it at the boy. "Guess you won't be needing your son anymore."

At the same time, Mrs. Hill was in the back, and she set off the alarm. Harris and Perez got the call. With no flashers or headlights on and a few minutes away, they pulled up to the front and eased the doors open. Ramos was pointing the gun at the teen. He was smiling, and said, "See you in hell." When he started to pull the trigger, he stopped and his face turned pale white. With a loud voice, he said, "You're dead, you're dead." He was pointing the gun at the window next to the door, screaming, "You're dead, you're dead. I killed you three years ago."

The Hills didn't move. All they could see was just Ramos pointing a gun at nothing. Then they saw Harris and Perez, but Ramos didn't pay any attention to anyone and just kept repeating, "You're dead, you're dead, don't come near me. I killed you both, you're dead."

Without warning, Ramos started shooting at nothing but kept repeating "Damn you, you're dead." When the shooting started, the bullets went through the store window. Harris and Perez were behind the doors of their car. They returned fire, and the Hills hit the floor as Ramos fell backward flat on his back with blood all over him from where he had been shot. Harris and Perez ran in, and Perez was next to Ramos so fast that he slipped but got the gun out of his hand. His hand was frozen around the handles, but he was still alive. Blood was running down his face, saying to both Perez and Harris, "They can't be alive. I killed them both, they're both dead." "Who is dead, Ramos, who?"

"The Syads. I killed them three years ago. They can't be alive. They're dead, they're dead."

Then his eyes fixed and were staring at nothing. Ramos breathed his last. Perez checked him out and told Harris that he was dead then closed his eyes.

"What the heck was he talking about?"

Mr. Hill then said, "He thought he saw someone standing there and kept repeating, 'You're dead, you're dead."

"Well, it looks like what goes around comes back at you. I'll call it in."

As Harris started to turn to leave, Perez told him, "Don't move." Harris froze. "Look down at your feet." As Harris looked down, there were two sets of footprints in blood on the floor, one of a man, the other smaller, like that of a boy. No other prints were around anywhere. As the men all looked at the bloody prints, a white light came through the blood. Then the light and the prints disappeared.

As they stared at the clean floor and each other, Mr. Hill said, "I said God would protect us. He keeps his word."

Harris didn't say anything and went on out to start the paperwork. He said, "That scrum bag is going to keep us up all night doing paperwork, while he's laying there dead."

Perez told the Hills to go to the back. "When this is over, we'll be back to board up the window." As he bent down over Ramos, he then realized that he just killed a man. As his stomach started to churn, his brain now realized he killed someone. He started to get sick. Without thinking, he asked God to forgive him for what he had done. As he said it, he looked in a glass door of a cola machine. He saw a man and a young boy smiling. Then they both nodded, turned, and their bodies became a flash of light. Perez blinked his eyes and saw Mr. Hill smiling and saying there was a better place they went to, across the bridge on the other side. Mr. Hill added, "Now they are with God in paradise."

By next morning, it was all over the news. The report stated that before Ramos died, he told the police he killed Mr. Syad and his son three years back. Nothing else was reported. For who would believe that after the paperwork was turned in, Perez asked the captain if he had a picture of the Syads, and the captain picked up a folder off his desk marked case closed and opened it and showed it to Perez. Perez thanked him. When he left, Harris met him.

"I'm not saying anything about those bloody prints. Hope you don't either."

"No, I won't."

"No one would believe."

Later that morning, Perez went back to the Hills, and everything was fine. All day people came from all over, saying, "Now we will take back our streets."

Perez asked Mr. Hill, "Why did you ever move here in the first place?"

Mr. Hill smiled. "As I said, God takes care of his flock. I had a dream. I bought this place to help the people, then a voice said, 'I will be with you every step of the way.'"

Perez returned home and hugged his mom. He said, "I think after last night, the south end and maybe the north end will change for a better place." Then retiring to his room, he prayed for the first time in a while, for the man and boy he saw in the cola case were the Syads. The next day was Sunday. He got dressed, and he and his mom went to the same church, the same one that helped her many years back. Patrolman Perez said a prayer for everyone. He smiled, for now he knew that one day, he would cross that bridge and go on to the other side to be with his real father in paradise.

CARVER HOUSE

The house sits on Carver Street at the edge of town, a beautiful example of American Queen Anne and Gothic combined, two large stories, and an attic with twelve-foot ceilings, built in 1882 by Thomas Evers Carver. But sad to say that even though the house is still in good shape, every door and window had been boarded up since 1960. That's when the last owner that lived there died, Thomas Carver's grandson, Samuel Carver. Samuel's only living heirs were his son and daughter. After fighting in the courts for control that lasted until Elizabeth died in 1990, Tim was now the only and last living heir to the Carver Estate and at seventy-five was in bad health.

Neither him nor Elizabeth would talk about the house. Neither got married. And they already had plenty. So Tim sold it as it stood at auction lock, stock, and barrel, including everything that was inside. The family never threw anything away. Most of the furniture was original to the house, which Thomas brought with him after he had the house built. Even then, the furniture was at least thirty years old and also a few pieces from the Queen Anne and Chippendale era that were made in New York. Most were high-end Victorian by John Belter and Meeks and other makers from the New York area, after the house was built, the largest in town. The attic was as tall as the rest of the rooms with twelve-foot ceilings and only four windows, one on each side of the house. But the windows were set high up near the roof line, very hard to see in or out. After the sale, the new owners, an architect, his wife, and their two small kids—their names Lewis and Sally Longtree and their twins Tony and Shirley, aged six—moved in.

Lewis worked in the capital and had his own company and six employees. Sally worked for a large corporation. But most of her work was from home. Twice a month, she would go in and give a bimonthly report. That way she could take care of the kids. Their house was only a forty-five-minute drive from his office. It was perfect. They bought the house at auction. All the windows and doors were still boarded up. They or no one else could see inside. So they bought it by only the word of some townsfolk and Eddie Forest, the groundskeeper. Even the coach house and side barn was full over the years. Eddie Forest was paid by the Carvers to mow and keep the yard clean, and when any of the nails came out of the boards, he had to put new ones back in. So Lewis asked Eddie if he would want to stay on and help inside and out. He would be paid well, and the job would be permanent. He agreed. He was twenty when Samuel Carver died.

So Tim and Elizabeth hired Eddie to mow and do repairs. To Eddie that was fine. He got paid well for part-time work. Eddie was in the house only once, and it was beyond his wildest dreams—it was full of furniture. Tim and Elizabeth never stepped foot inside or on the property again and just paid to have it cleaned and paid for the taxes and insurance. Lewis and Sally went overboard, paying twice as much as the appraisal said it would bring. Once the deeds were signed and Tim received his money, he left town, and left no forwarding address. His last words to the Longtrees were, "Good luck, you're going to need it."

That afternoon, the Longtrees, with Eddie, stood in front of the house. All had hammers and saws, ready to take the boards down and let the sun shine in. It would be the first time in fifty years, and even the townsfolk joined in. It was a beautiful house, but it made the rest of the town look bad. Then *bang*, the boards started to fall on the porch. Lewis put the key in the lock, turned it, and it opened as if it was a new lock. The door was hard to open. It squeaked, but after a few tugs, it swung free. The smell after all those years, they had to put mask on so they could breathe. Then someone yelled, "Hey, we got the back door off, this place needs to be aired out."

Afraid the mice or rats might have eaten the wiring, they rented fans and an electric generator, put a fan at the front door, and turned it on. The smell was terrible. While the fan was running, the rest of the boards were taken down. It took almost three hours. Around 4:00 p.m., the drapes were pulled back and the windows were open after fifty years. The house now had sunshine all throughout. The rooms were large, twelve-foot ceilings, the entry twenty by thirty, with double solid golden oak stairs, every door, window, floor, all the moldings were solid oak, nothing painted. The large gas chandeliers had been electrified. Every room was filled with furniture, oil paintings. Handblown glass everywhere. When you looked no matter what room, you went back in time. Fireplaces were in every room, stone, marble, oak, some went almost to the ceilings, and the the ceilings were heavily molded in ornate plaster; every wall was beautiful with wallpaper or hand-painted murals.

As they and the townsfolk walked through, no one could believe their eyes. Eighteen chairs around the dining room table. It was the largest room in the house. Two large formal parlors, one for the man of the house, the other for the lady, even on the parlor table was a box of cigars. When Lewis tried to pick one up, it just turned to dust. There were dust and cobwebs everywhere. After looking around and talking with some of the neighbors, Lewis said, "This town is in need of fixing up, but we need to have some cash to spend."

The town was almost broke, but the folks had nice homes. Some like the Carver house have been in the same family for over one hundred years. He and Sally called a meeting. Lewis said, "I'm an architect. Help me clean up the inside and out, make it livable for me and my family. I'll make this town a tourist attraction. You have just one main street. From what I've been told, all these homes are at least ninenty years old or older. I'll help you fix up your homes and pay for it, put up a sign at the edge of town saying the town that didn't change in time."

So within a few weeks, the place was cleaned from top to bottom. Even the furniture was cleaned. Most of the drapes were OK, at least for the time being. It took all spring and even up to the first snow. Every day, to get all new electric, plumbing, and two furnaces, with Lewis's input and contacts, he had a new kitchen, more baths, and he opened the carriage house for cars. Eddie lived upstairs, and he had one bedroom, living room with kitchen and bath. It was also very large, and they were hoping to have an old-fashioned Christmas and invite the whole town. And next spring that's when the town, he hoped, would get back on the map. Besides the Carver house, there were others, small to large, all different styles, made in unique ways. Lewis paid to have their houses fixed up. Painted whatever it took, and the town was grateful.

Around Thanksgiving, they sold all the Queen Anne and Chippendale furniture. It brought more than the house did. The Longtrees were good people. They split the sale, they kept half, and the other half was split in two parts—one-fourth went to the school for computers and other items so the kids could be in the twenty-first century. The other fourth was split between the townsfolk, those that owned homes. They could restore the inside and hope in the near future they could have an open house. Also, part of the sale went to his employees. They helped him on the house. Also, Eddie was included. They all agreed that this town would be a so-called family town. No matter who would live there, it was one for all and all for one.

Thanksgiving was warm that year, so the people, like the Pilgrims, had a feast. The street was blocked off, and the whole town joined in. Around Christmas, Sally asked Tony if he was big enough to go to the attic and turn on the stars. There were four stars, and one was put in each window. Within twenty minutes, Tony came back, not saying a word.

"Tony, did you turn on the stars?" Sally asked.

"No. They were already on."

"Already on? Shirley, did you turn them on?"

"No, Mommy."

"Are you sure, Tony? This is not Halloween. Are you playing a trick on us?"

"No, Mommy. It was dark when I went in, then the stars, they all came on. One at a time. I thought I saw something looking at me."

"Well, there, it's all right. Must have been a short. And the shadow must have been from the lights. I'll have Daddy to look at it, OK? Now let's go and have some hot choco. Daddy will be home in a few minutes and come up and say good night."

"Will Daddy check out the attic tonight when he gets in?"

"Yes, I'll have him to, and he will let us know at breakfast what he found."

When Lewis got in, it was around eight. He said, "Sorry to be late, the closing of that contract for the office building took longer than I thought. Kids are tucked in?"

"Yes," Sally said, "by the way, Lewis, before we retire, let's go to the attic. Tony said he saw something. And the lights, those Christmas stars, they came on by themselves. One at a time. Could it be a short?"

"We'll see. And what's for dinner?"

"Sorry, roast warmed over."

"That's fine. After I eat, I'll take a look. So within the hour all looks OK to me. I'll keep an eye on it, but we have all new electric. Yes, and a new kitchen and three new bathrooms. Hope there are no more problems. Well, so far we're lucky. We had sprayed insulation. That made the house even warmer and cooler when it's hot outside. These outside walls are eighteen inches thick, solid stone. The house was in good condition, just some TLC."

"Yes, except for the attic. The kids would love to have that as a playroom. It's large, so they can invite all their friends over, we did promise."

"Yes, I know, hon."

"Lewis, Tony said earlier, I forgot to tell you. He said it's cold up there. He saw his breath there yesterday."

"Sally, it's an attic, no heat. Once it's finished with heat, it will be fine. So can we retire? I'm tired. And I have a full day tomorrow, have a meeting with your boss for another building. That will take most of the day."

It was the weekend before Christmas on a Saturday. Everybody was invited to the Carver house for a first reborn Christmas party. The Longtrees had everything to eat, brought in from the capital with the money from the sale of the furniture. They could afford it. The sale did pay off the house, all repairs, and lots of extras to spend and put enough aside for the kids' future. At around seven, the party was winding down. The coworkers had left to go to other parties, and only a few neighbors remained. They all pitched in to clean up the place. Any leftovers were given to anyone who wanted them. The kids and a few of their friends were upstairs. Shirley and the girls were in her room. Just Tommy from next door with Tony.

"Hey, Tony, why are there three locks on the door to the attic?"

Tony gave a look and, in a creepy voice, said, "It's to keep the boogeyman locked up. But it's not locked."

"Oh!"

"He did not like it up there, so he ran away. Do you want to go up and play?"

"Yeah."

"OK, but it's cold up there. No heat, but Dad will fix it for us when it gets warm. Then we can have all you guys over."

"Can we take a peek anyway, even in the cold?"

"Sure."

And the boys went up. Tony flipped on a switch, and four lights came on. Once upstairs, Tommy asked, "Tony, why are the walls like this and not like the walls downstairs?"

"It's an attic."

"What's in your attic?"

"Just boxes and Christmas lights and junk. We have the barn in the back for all that junk. So this will be ours when it's finished."

Then, without thinking, Tony hit the wooden panels on the wall a number of times. "See, no boogeyman."

As fast as the words *boogeyman* came out of Tony's mouth, moaning and crying came from the other side of the wall. The boys looked at each other and started screaming and running down the stairs, knocking each other over. That's when the adults downstairs heard the screaming. All took off upstairs. The boys were white with fright and couldn't say a word. When they calmed down, they told the adults what happened. Lewis and two friends went up and checked it out. Nothing. All they could hear was the wind howling through some cracks that had yet to be fixed. It just started snowing outside.

"With the wind in this attic, at their age or even ours, hearing this wind at night, I might run."

They all laughed. When they came back down, they told the boys it was just the wind. Both boys just shook their heads.

"It wasn't the wind. Dad, why are there three locks on the door?"

"I don't know."

"Why are these rooms so big?"

"It's to keep the big furniture in."

"But, Dad, this furniture can't fit up in the attic."

"Well, then, it's a story. No, a mystery. Then we will check it out."

"You mean it?"

"Sure, we have to fix the attic for you kids. Next winter, it will be warm up there."

"Well," Tommy said, "Good night, and to all, have a merry Christmas."

"Same to all of you. And thanks for coming over. Well, it's way after nine. Time for bed, you two."

"Gee, can we stay up and watch TV? It's Saturday. And it's Christmas."

"Well, all right."

"For a little while, I'll help Mom finish up. You two, go and get some hot choco. But don't spill it. Wednesday is Christmas. What about the puppy and kitten?"

"I'll pick them up Tuesday. Victor and his family are taking care of them."

"Do you have everything, including the litter box?"

"All put away in the attic. I doubt after tonight they won't slip up there and check things out."

At least for a while, nothing else was said about the attic, just sugar plums and gifts going through the kids' heads. Wednesday morning came, and the kids were downstairs at the break of dawn. Eddie had the puppy and kitten ready to bring over after breakfast. Lewis and Sally were fixing sausage and eggs when the rear doorbell rang. It was Eddie. Eddie became a grandfather figure to the kids. Both Lewis's and Sally's parents passed away long before they were married.

"Are the kids up?" Eddie asked.

"Oh yeah. We heard them. They're under the tree, checking things out. They know they can't open the gifts until after breakfast. Eddie, have a seat."

"How did the two little ones do last night?"

"Fine, both slept in bed with me and cuddled up together. OK, kids, come and eat. Eddie is joining us."

When they all sat down, Lewis said a prayer for all, including the town praying for peace. That's what Christmas is all about.

"You know, Lewis, I bet this is the only time a prayer has been given in this house."

"Eddie, why do you say that?"

"Well, from what my aunt and uncle told me, they never did. Although he never went to church, his wife did. I'm talking about Thomas, not Samuel. And the kids did and Samuel and his wife. And you know Tim, they all went to church. But they told me no prayers were ever said at the table."

After breakfast, they all went to the parlor where the tree was. And the kids had a free-for-all as the adults laughed. Memories of their childhood raced through their heads. When all was said and done, two small boxes were brought out and given to the kids. Tony opened his first. A dog collar and chain fell to the floor, and Tony's mouth was wide open. He said, "I got a dog, I got a dog. Where is he?"

Finally, Shirley got hers open, and saw three round balls with bells inside. At first, she didn't know what the balls were for. Then she saw a picture of a kitten playing with them. Pandemonium broke out. Both were jumping up and down, and asking, "Where? Where are they?"

Then Eddie got up and smiled. "I'll be right back," he said. When Eddie left, the kids said, "Mom, Dad, we didn't get anything for Eddie."

"Oh, yes, we did. You know that old beat-up truck he uses? Well, we asked him what he was going to do with it. That money we gave him, it's in savings. When he retires, in which he said he hoped it never would happen, but it would help. Said he just would have to keep his truck and keep it repaired. So we watch him. There is a truck. Every time he and I would go to the capital, he would look at it, and his eyes would get as big as yours. When he comes back with your pets, then we will show him his new red truck. And remember, you are responsible for them."

When Eddie returned, he had a small puppy and kitten. The kids went wild. Although the puppy and kitten at first were scared to death, Mom and Dad calmed them both down. And all listened to Eddie how to raise them.

Eddie said, "You see, I used to have both. But when I got older and had to work, they both died. So I never got any more although I fed the feral cats. That's what you call them if they go wild or out in the streets. It's the people's fault. Once the kittens and, sometimes, dogs, grow to be adults, they just turn them loose. So I feed the outside cats all the time. Now I don't think there are any around here, but there's a lot in the city."

"Eddie, can you do us a favor?"

"Sure, what is it?"

"People are coming over later. Could you move a truck out of the driveway?"

"What's a truck doing in the driveway?"

"Someone left it here with the keys. Here you go."

"OK, be back in a second."

"OK, kids, let's see Eddie's reaction."

When Eddie opened the door, he saw a large card on the wheel with all their pictures on it, saying "Merry Christmas, Eddie." For the first time since his parents died, Eddie broke down and cried. It was just the Longtrees and Eddie plus the pup and kitten. All had a wonderful Christmas dinner. Eddie gave them all a gift, saying, "You're the family I never had." Then they all hugged. The pup ran into the entry and tried to go up the stairs. Within a minute, he came running into the dining room, yelping, with his tail between his legs.

"Do dogs protect their owners, Dad?"

"Sure, some have to be trained. For others, it comes natural. What are you two going to name them?"

"We have to talk it over, won't we, sis?"

"Yes, but they have to have nice names."

"Well, they are yours. You name them, you take care of them," said Eddie. "Folks, I got to go, it snowed last night, and it's a long drive away."

"Eddie, I have have nothing else to do, let's do it together and talk."

Later that night, Tony put the pup on the bed, but the pup kept whining. When Tony awoke, the pup was gone. As he looked around, the door was wide open. He remembered he had closed the door. When he looked out, down at the end of the hallway was the pup, sitting and staring at the attic door. So he went and picked the pup up. And as he started to turn, he heard the same noise, moaning and crying. The pup heard it also and started to growl. As fast as he could, he ran into his room and made sure this time the door was shut. He looked in his arms at the pup.

"You're a good watchdog. I'm going to name you Fearless."

Then he put Fearless under the covers with him. Shirley named the kitten Missy because she was a little lady. Both of the pets got along great even though at times they would cuddle up together when the kids were at school. Missy would avoid the attic door. Fearless would growl, and his hair would stand on end. When he was near it, Shirley never heard a thing even after Tony told her. She would say, "It's all in your head."

The following Monday, the kids were in school. Sally was cleaning the bedrooms when she had a strange feeling that someone or something was watching her. "Must be Fearless or Missy," she thought. As she left Tony's room, she noticed she could see her breath and she was ice cold. The door to the attic was wide open. Out of nowhere, Fearless came from Shirley's room, growling and with his hair standing on end. He was not moving and was just staring at the attic door. Then she felt warm again, and Fearless turned and walked up to her and sat between her legs. But he kept staring at the door. Then Missy came out, looked toward the door, and as little as she was, she came running and sat next to Fearless.

"Well, you two do make and odd couple," she said as she picked both up. "It's an old house, things happen."

But when she got to the stairs to go down, the door was still open, and all three heard moaning and crying. This time she knew it wasn't the wind. Over the next few months, the kids were busy in school and Fearless and Missy were growing fast. Fearless was a mixed breed, part German shepherd and Malamute and collie. He started to lose that cute puppy hair and weighed about twenty pounds. Still, when the kids were gone, they would play and sleep together—a perfect odd couple.

Then in late March, Lewis told all he was ready to start on the attic soon. Saturday morning, Eddie was there. They all started to go up into the attic when Tony stopped, Fearless stopped in front of them all, hair standing on end, growling and showing his teeth.

"What's going on here? I don't want to go up there. Fearless won't let me, Sally, do you know something I don't know?"

"OK, let's all go back down to the kitchen. I'll fix some coffee and tea."

At the table, Sally fixed some tea for the kids and coffee for the rest.

"Let me tell this the way I like to tell it, so please don't butt in. It started at Christmas. At the party, Tony and Tommy heard what they thought was moaning and crying. You said it was the wind. After the Christmas break, kids went back to school. The only ones here at the house were me, Fearless, and Missy. On a number of occasions, I noticed that Fearless would sit at the attic door with his hair standing on end, growling and showing his teeth. Missy wouldn't go near the door. That's when the moaning and crying started. When I first heard it, I said, 'Oh, it's the wind,' but there was no wind. So I went up to check it out. Fearless went before me and stopped at the head of the stairs. I thought he was going to attack something, then I stopped, looked around. Nothing. We went back down, it started again. This went on for at least an hour. Finally, I made Fearless stay and went up alone. The sound was coming from the center in the back of the attic, what we call the square. It looks like someone built something but never finished it.

"I've noticed other things. Tony locks his door at night, I don't."

Shirley hushed. Then she said, "Oh, it's all in Tony's head. He told me he hears things, and his door comes open all by itself. He's just trying to scare me. It's not working. My door never opens by itself. It's afraid of Missy. She will scratch whoever it is."

"So you think this place is haunted?"

"I didn't say that, just what I told you."

"OK, we're all here. Eddie, tell them, even the kids, all you know about this place and leave nothing out."

"Well, OK, here goes. Thomas Evers Carver, one day, got off the train in 1880. There was a train that went through here. On its way to the capital. The depot was still there. You know where it's at, it's used as a town hall. Not large, heck, this town is not large, anyway. He bought this track of land, five acres. And there were Italian stonemasons working in the capital. He went to see them. He had no blueprint for the house. It just gave them an idea, wanted it very fancy with eighteen-inch-thick stonewalls for the outside, also large rooms with twelve-foot ceilings including the attic. He was very precise about the attic. The door had to be at the end of the hallway. The hallways had to be very wide and also the stairs to the attic—only four windows, one on each side, they were larger than most attics, but these had to sit as high as the roof, so it's hard to see in or out. Told them how many rooms, oak all inside, very ornate everywhere. The house had to sit in the center of the track, the carriage house and barn in the back. A driveway went up to and half circle to the front door. Also there was a side door. The driveway then went on to the carriage house and barn.

"The only thing, according to the blueprint that the head Italian or the boss man drew up, that was odd was what was in the attic. It was that square in the back part of the attic. And one more thing, you can't hear anyone walking on the floor in the attic. Those Italian boys were good. They had to have all the floor in the attic just like the wall all made out of stone. Then wood planks were put over the stones so the floor is around twelve inches less thick than the walls. But they were soundproof, and it took some doings, but it was done. We call it soundproofing today. Why? Why all that? I don't know, it took two years. They worked every day but Sunday. Once the frame was up, the coach house and barn were finished first. So they used those buildings to do all the carvings and making the molds for the ceilings and around some walls.

"When it was finished, Mr. Carver came back. Not once did he come back during the construction to review it. He liked what he saw. Everything was ready to move in, drapes, wallpaper. Only thing was missing was the furniture. So within a month, boxcars came into the depot. How many? I don't know. All the workers and even the townsfolk at the time, including my great-great-aunt and uncle, unloaded everything from small to large. It took days. Same man in charge of the house was in charge of placing all the furniture, everything down to the last detail. A few pieces of furniture was placed in the attic like someone was living up there. Then a few days passed, and luggage arrived with their clothes and personal needs.

"Then sometime during the night, Mr. Carver, his wife, and kids arrived. No one knew in the town that they had arrived until Mr.

Carver knocked on my aunt's and uncle's door. He hired them to take care of the house, cook, clean up but they were only allowed downstairs and work in the yard and take everyone to and from the capital. It was strange that no one was allowed upstairs for no reason. His excuse was that it was private bedchambers. They cleaned up their own beds, so no one ever went up. Also, there was always one member of the family that would stay behind when the rest would go to the capital. Mr. Carver, he helped with the town and gave the locals money, paid to have those large stones for the main street.

"Before it was just dirt and mud everywhere. He did OK with the town. Through him, the town grew. His family went to church, he never did. According to Aunt Polly, no grace was ever said at the table. His aunt and uncle had to be out of the house at six sharp and back in no earlier than eight in the morning. He told them he came into a great sum of money when his parents died. They had businesses in England and Italy. So a few years before they died, they sold all their businesses. There, and he was the only child, he got it all. He invested in land all around New York City and around the Philadelphia area. He lived in the house till his death in 1902. They say he was buried in a solid bronze and oak casket imported from Italy. It was the first time the townsfolk ever saw him in church. That was at his funeral. In 1907, his wife died, and everything was left to his two kids, Samuel and Louise. Louise took her half, left town, and was never heard from since.

"Samuel's mother was buried in the same type of casket as Thomas. When they were alive, they bought a very large tract of land and gave it to the town for a cemetery. That great big iron fence, they had it put up, and all the plots were drawn out. They gave each plot to each family of the town in case they wished to be buried there. They were funny people. Today they would be called weird. But they gave to the town and the people, so the townsfolk and my aunt and uncle respected their wishes.

"The same continued on with Samuel. Samuel was twenty-three when his father died. When my aunt and uncle died, Samuel asked their son and his wife to take over. They all were paid very well. Then Samuel got married to a girl from New York, and they had two kids, Tim and Elizabeth. She died when the kids were teens. Then Samuel died in 1960. Both kids never married. They still lived in the house for a short time. The money was split even. They were wealthy even without this house and all the furnishings. They let my aunt and uncle go. They were up in their years. They had one child. When my mom and dad died, they lived in the capital. I moved here. They offered a job to Joe, but unlike his parents, he was no maid to no one. So they offered the job to me. Then they ended up in court over the house. Elizabeth moved back to New York and died there. Tim moved to the capital until now. So you know the rest. The town tried to get Tim to turn it over to the town as a museum. He flat out said no."

"So are they buried here?"

"Oh yeah. Funny, though, that they're buried together in the family plot, but there's one vacant grave, it's between Mr. Carver and his wife. You think they would be buried side by side."

"Well, one thing's for sure. I'm having no ghost running me out of my home."

"Way to go, Mommy."

"Hush, Shirley."

"Mommy, why is it that you and Tony hear those things, but me and Daddy and Eddie don't? I knew I should have kept quiet."

"Well, I'm glad you did. I've wondered about the attic the way those slabs of boards are put up there. I know the wood is at least one hundred years old. Maybe it was to help keep the house warm. You know, come to think of it, it doesn't look like those Italians put it up—too crude. Well, I'll tell you what we're going to do. You kids go outside with your pets and play. Sally, you fix us a good dinner. Eddie and I are going to take those boards down once and for all.

We should find something if there is something to find. Let's get started. Tony, are you sure you don't want to help?"

"No!"

"OK. Just asking. Let's go, Eddie, we have all the tools we need. Well, where shall we start first?"

"How about here? Looks like this is where they might have ended their work. Some of these nails are already coming out."

"Yeah! Due to the shrinkage of the wood, this board is coming off easy. It's off. What the! What the heck is this, wallpaper?"

"Looks like it. Let's take some more off. Let's be careful, we may not have to do too much work up here after all."

Within a half hour, the front boards were off and put in a pile.

"I don't believe this, wait till Sally sees this. Hey, Sally," he said as he ran down the stairs. "Come on up, stop what you're doing. We've uncovered a masterpiece."

When she stepped into the attic, her mouth opened so wide, she could not speak. "It's beautiful, I have never seen anything like it before."

As their fingers touched the wall, tears started to run down her face. The wall was a mural painting of the town. The background was the capital. The artist, whoever he or she was, had to look out the window to see. At first it looked like a picture was taken of the town and the surroundings then blown up and pasted on the wall. But no, this was all hand painted. What was behind the other walls? Within another hour, with all three taking the boards off very gently, everywhere, whoever did it, had painted what they could see.

"Lewis, all those painting and drawings all over the house, all have just a D on them. Do you think it's done by the same person?"

"Could be. Oh my."

"Lewis, I think you had better see this."

"What?"

"There. A door here opens to that square. It's locked. No key."

"Can we open it?"

"I'll be right back. I have a few keys that are old. Maybe one will fit."

Within ten minutes, Eddie was back.

"Let's see. So far, none. Wait, it turns."

The key unlocked the door.

"Lewis, it's your house. You do the honors."

The door sung outward, wide and tall. Totally dark inside.

"Wait, I'll get an oil lamp from the bedroom."

When she returned, she lit it.

"OK, now, let's have a look and see," said Lewis. "Oh my God."

"What is it, Lewis?" Sally asked.

"Sally, I think you should stay out. Go and get some more lamps. You help, Eddie."

When they returned, three more lamps were lit.

"Don't drop the lamps when you come in."

"Oh my! What have we uncovered?"

At the edge of the back wall was a very large bronze and oak casket, with tubes of paint and brushes, and dried flowers. It was a room with a large chair and books, even a half-completed oil was still on the easel.

"What is this?"

"I don't know."

"Is there anyone inside?"

"I'm not opening it."

"It's been here for a long, long time. Is that why Elizabeth didn't want to sell the place? Wait, here's a book leaning on the lid."

As Lewis opened it, it started out. "The confessions of a father."

"Lewis, what are we going to do?"

"Only one thing to do, call the police."

"Are you sure you want to do this? So far it's only a casket and papers scattered around."

As Lewis picked up the book, he said, "Let's go and have something to eat and talk it over. If no one is in the casket, no problem. Maybe these notes will help. I'm locking the door. Don't want the kids up here. Eddie, do you know anything about all this?"

"No, I don't know nothing. Maybe this casket was meant for Samuel."

"Then why was it brought up here? Concealed and not put in the barn. I'll bet that's what it was for."

"For what?"

"The empty grave between Thomas and his wife."

"Oh my. Do you suppose someone is in that casket? Sally, when will dinner be ready?"

"Ready now. Pork roast. All I have to do is fix a salad and get the cola on ice."

"Set the table, I'll get the kids. Eddie, go and lock the door to the attic."

During dinner, Shirley kept saying, "Tell us what you found in the attic."

"Oh, just some paintings behind those boards."

"Can we see?"

"Not today. It's very messy up there, rusty nails all over the floor. You just have to wait"

"Any crying?"

"No, Tony, no crying. See, I told you. Shirley, be quiet. Tony, both of you be quiet. We have been up there all day, you two. If you're finished, go and play outside or watch TV. We have to discuss some things."

"Come on, Shirley. When we leave like this, it's adult stuff."

"Well, they're right about that. Now what are we going to do?"

"Lewis, let's put this off until tomorrow. It will give us the night to think things over. If there's a body in the casket, one, who is it? And two, was he or she killed, or what?"

"Tomorrow then. The square is locked and the door."

"Well, OK. That's a night. I'm going to turn in."

"Don't stay awake thinking about what's upstairs. It's been here for over one hundred years. One more day is not going to matter."

Then Lewis sat down in the library and started to read. It was a diary from Thomas when he lived in New York. The more he read, the more his mouth became wide open. When Sally came in later, he was crying. After wiping his eyes, he said, "You're not going to believe this. It's a diary from Thomas Carver, all the way back to when they lived in New York. I'm at where he's writing and praying at the same time. It's unbelievable."

As he put the diary down, he told Sally what he had read.

"You mean there is?"

"Yes, according to this."

Then without saying a word, he picked up the phone and called a friend on the police force and just told him to try to contact Ted Carver. It had something to do with the house and that he must see him, if he can help find him, that it was very important. Jimmy said he will make a few phone calls. All that evening, they both took turns reading the diary. Then they had finished.

"What are we going to do?"

"Well, for one thing, if this is true, they would have to convict a dead man for not notifying the police for a person that might have had a stroke or heart attack. Unless Ted knows something about it."

"Oh my! If Ted knew, would he still sell the house? Maybe, he's in bad health, him smoking all his life. We'll wait till tomorrow. If we don't hear from Ted by then, we'll open it and see for ourselves."

"OK, wow!"

It was after eleven. The kids, as they went through the kitchen to the family room, they were asleep. Missy was on top of Fearless, and they were between the kids. Without waking them, they picked them up. The two little ones woke up, and they all went upstairs to bed. Around two, Fearless sat up in bed. He looked at the door as it opened. He started to growl, but then his tail started wagging in a minute. He's at the attic door. It was unlocked and wide open. As he turned, Tony was behind him, eyes wide open, but sound asleep. Nothing was said as both of them climbed the stairs, and went straight for the square and stood in front of the door. The door then opened without the use of the key. It was pitch-black inside. The only light in the attic was the moonlight that shined through the windows.

Without blinking his eyes, he went to the end of the casket where the large chair was. On the chair was a key. He picked it up and he and Fearless left and went back downstairs to his parents' bedroom and stood at the foot of the bed. Within seconds, Fearless started to whine.

"Fearless, what the!"

Lewis woke up. As Lewis opened his eyes, Sally turned on the table lamp. Tony was standing at the foot of the bed, holding out a key, wide-eyed but still asleep. Was he sleepwalking? He had never done this before. As they got out of bed, that's when they noticed the key.

"Is that the key to the door?"

"No, it's here."

Then Tony woke up and started crying and jumped on the bed. And then he hugged his dad.

"I saw the ghost. It came into my room and made me and Fearless go up in the attic. There's a casket in the square, the ghost is in it. I saw him."

"Tony, you had a bad dream. The attic door is locked and there is no casket in the square."

"Yes, there is. This key opens it. He made me pick it up off the chair and bring it to you."

"Lewis, now did he—"

Before Sally could finish, Lewis got out of bed, just in his underwear and looked out into the hall. The door was open, and lights were on upstairs. Within a few minutes, they were dressed. All went up, and everything Tony said was true. The door to the square was wide open, and all four oil lamps were lit up. As they all looked inside, Missy rubbed against Sally's legs, and she let out a scream. Then she saw Missy. She and Fearless seemed not one bit afraid, but they stayed together.

"Now what?"

"Tony, take them out."

"I want to stay. The ghost is trying to tell us something."

"OK, are you man enough to stay?"

"Fearless is here. He'll protect us all."

"OK. Let's see if the key works to unlock the casket. Where do you unlock it?"

"Try running your fingers around it. Dad, how big is this?"

"Well, it looks like it's over seven feet or more. Wow! I think I found it." *Click.* "It works. Is everybody ready?"

"Hey, what's going on?"

"Shirley, hun, pick up Missy and please go back to bed."

"No way. You're ghost hunting."

"There are no such things as ghosts."

"I'm going to watch. Wow! A casket. Boy is it big! Can we use it for Halloween?"

"Shirley, this is not funny."

"Well, we're all in this as a family. Sorry, Mommy. Is there someone in it?"

"Shirley, shut up, and let Dad open it."

"Dead people can't hurt you, can they, Dad?"

"Is everyone ready? Before I open it, remember, if there is a body in there, it will smell very bad. So put your sleeve over your nose. OK, here goes. The lid came up without a squeak.

"Oh my God! Is that human?"

"Yes, from what Thomas Carver's diary says, it's his son. That's him. He had a form of two diseases. One what we call the elephant disease, the other was gigantism. It made you grow very tall. His name was David. He had both. But look at him, he looks like he just died. Was he embalmed? If he was, then I bet Thomas and the family did it."

"He had the money, he could have paid someone to do it. Shirley, don't touch him, touching him may do damage with this fresh air. He may start to turn to dust like the Bible says, hun."

"Dad," Tony said.

"Yes, son?"

"You know, Daddy, he may want us to touch him, to show us he's not a freak."

"True. Besides his family, who else would have touched him back then?"

Then Lewis leaned over David's body and put his hand on his face. When he did, he started to cry and started saying the Lord's Prayer. Then all joined in. One by one, they touched him. Tony picked up Fearless and showed him David. Fearless's ears folded down as if he knew. Shirley did the same with Missy. She looked at David and gave a small cry.

"Look, here's a notebook with handwriting in it. It looks like Thomas's writing. Let's go downstairs, I'm not sleepy now."

"Can we have what they call a wake, Dad?"

"We'll see. Better close the lid, hun."

"No. It will stay open for now. It's been closed too long. I think David would want the people to know about him and the art that he has done. We have to talk to Tim and then the police."

"What about David, Dad?"

"Once this is over and we get some answers, we will have a service for him in the church. Then we will bury him between his dad and mom. I reckon that's what he would have wanted. We'll have an open house twice a year for David. Let everyone come in to see his artwork. It may bring better understanding with the general public about these special people, for it's what's inside that counts."

Ding dong.

"Who's at the back door?"

Eddie said, "Sorry, folks, something woke me up. I saw lights on in the attic. What's going on?"

"Fix some coffee and tea. It's already seven. Wow, just fix us all some breakfast. Everyone, wash your hands good. Come on. I'll show you."

When they returned, breakfast was ready.

"I don't believe it. He looks—"

"Yes, we know, like he just died."

"I've read of strange things before, but I never thought it would happen to me or this house. That's why Elizabeth didn't want to sell, but why did Tim?"

"Well, we just have to wait to hear from Jimmy."

They waited all day and night, but they got no word during the waiting. They went back to the attic. So far, everything seemed fine.

"You know, this Thomas was ashamed of his son, and look at the beautiful artwork he did. Even then the world would have loved him. You know, Sally, I think Thomas might have been ashamed of himself. In the diary we read, the last part was missing. Yes. This is the last part. It's a farewell prayer to his son. That's why he left it in the casket with him. It's Monday morning already, and I have to go to work and take the kids to school. You two come here. I want you two to listen and listen well. Neither one of you are to say anything about what's up in the attic about David. Anything. Do both of you understand? It's a secret, and no one is to know, at least for now. By tomorrow, everybody will know!"

At the office, "Hello, yes, Jimmy. Sorry you missed me at the house. Did you get in touch with Tim Carver? You did. What did he say? Here's his phone number. OK. Look, Jimmy, I'm going to call you back after I talk with Tim. I'm going to need some advice. Yes, it involves police work. But you're with the city. I may have to go to the state police because we don't have a police force here. Yeah, you're right. Maybe the county sheriff. I'll let you know, and thanks. Well, just as well, get this on the road."

After about ten rings, someone answered. "Hello, hello, Mr. Carver? Yes, this is Lewis Longtree."

"Oh, yes. What can I do for you?"

"Well, let's say for starters you can come over to the house. We got to talk about something."

"Mr. Longtree, you bought that house as is. It's yours now."

"Yes, I know that. What we're going to talk about is a dead body. Your great uncle David."

"Uncle David? I have no Uncle David. And what do you mean by a dead body?"

"Then you don't know. Know what, I'm going to tell you over the phone, but you are coming to the house one way or the other. We found a dead body in the attic."

"A dead body in the attic? You're nuts. I've been up there. There is nothing."

"Mr. Carver, I'm going to make this very simple. You know that square that's in the attic?

"Yes, it looks out of place. Yes, but I don't know anything about it."

"You don't?"

"No!"

"Well, it's a tomb. You're uncle is in it. He has been for around one hundred years. And no, I'm not drinking. I don't drink. I'm expecting you at the house at six tonight, or the police will be knocking on your door."

Around six, Ted rang the bell.

"Hello, Ted, please come in. You know Sally, and Eddie will be in a few minutes."

"Look, Mr. Longtree, what you said over the phone. I know nothing about anybody named David."

"Well, have coffee."

"Boy, you sure have done a lot to this place."

"Yes, we have. Let's talk in the kitchen, then we're going to show you the attic. Here comes Eddie."

When all got settled in, they talked. "Ted, what do you know about this house and your family?"

"Probably Eddie knows as much as I do."

"Why did you and Elizabeth fight over the house?"

"Well, for me. It was too big to live in. Neither of us got married. I don't know why she didn't want to sell. I told her let someone else take over. We just put a clause in the deed that the house can't be torn down or altered to make apartments or convert it into a rooming house. She just kept saying, 'They will find out. Our name would be mud.' I still don't know what she meant by that."

"What about the attic?"

"What about it? It's an attic. Large but an attic."

"Do you know anything about the square—that's what we call it—and those boards that are nailed all over the wall?"

"They both were there before we were born. I asked Dad. He just said it was part of the foundation of the house."

"When I bought the house, you said when you left, 'Good luck, you're going to need it.' What did you mean by that?"

"OK, I'll tell you. As far back as I can remember, I heard things. Moaning and crying. It was coming from the attic. And other things. I even heard the crying the night Dad died. At first I thought it was the wind or the settling of the house. After a while, I paid no attention to it."

"The first bedroom to the left?"

"Oh, that was my room. Elizabeth's was the next one. My door would come open by itself. I thought it was the wind. It would even blow the attic door open."

"Why?" The three looked at the attic door.

"I don't know. I asked my dad, he would never answer. Now you tell me what's going, on or I'm leaving. You can call whoever you want. You said the police. You call them. It had better be a good one."

"Well, we shall see, Tim. We're going to show you something. Your sister might have found the answers. Let's all go up to the attic."

As they entered, Tim exclaimed. "Wow! What's this?"

"You don't know? All those paintings and drawings signed with a D. That stands for David, your great-uncle."

"I said I don't have a uncle named David."

"Then do you know anything about all this? This painting all over the wall?"

"No, I've never seen this before. It's unbelievable. Who did it?"

"Come in. The square, I'll show you."

As they entered, Tim asked, "What's a casket doing up here?"

"Look inside."

"Oh my God. Who . . . what is it?"

"That, Mr. Carver, is your uncle David. Thomas Evers Carver's third child. That's why they moved here. He was ashamed of his own son. Who, by the way, painted all this and those paintings and drawings that Thomas had framed and hung. He wasn't ashamed of them, just his son who painted them."

"I'm telling you the truth. These boards were covered before I was born. Dad just said it was to keep the cold out."

"Did your dad know?"

"I don't know. He might have. You know, my sister might have known or she had found out. It could be that's why she didn't want to sell this place. David there had that elephant disease, that's what it is. I've seen people with it on TV. Different, but living normal lives, so to speak."

"Well, we found Thomas's diary, and in it he told everything from the time David was born. He was born normal. It was about one and a half years old when he started to get bigger and started having those tumors. The doctors told Thomas what his son had and what would happen as he grew older. According to the diary, David talked normal, and he had this ability to read. But with his hand, he could not hold the pen to write. He signed those oil paintings and drawings with just a D, but he could hold a paintbrush and had an eye and a keen mind. He could copy anything on paper, even the drawing, he could, but he could not hold a pen to write. He died, and they put him here. He ordered three caskets, all the same, but his was almost eight feet long. David was seven feet seven inches tall. The last six months before he died, that large tumor was pressing very heavy on his brain. It started making him very mad. They had to put three locks on his door just to protect himself. At the end, he could not walk. Or hardly move, it also said. He just lay there. He was fed with a spoon. His casket was stored in New York, so they sent for it. It was in a box brought here and taken out of the crate by night by the family members and taken to the attic, placed in the square. He went to the capital to an undertaker. They paid him well to come here and do his work. The same undertaker that took care of Thomas and his wife. So something happened. David is like Lenin in Moscow. But not in a glass case. We're going to have to call the police. You're going to have to talk to them. But once this is over, he will be buried between his father and mother."

"So that's why there was an empty grave. We thought it was for Dad. But he said no, his spot was next to his mother. My aunt, she moved back to New York. Never heard from her again. Although Dad said this house should never be sold. Maybe Elizabeth knew or just wanted to do what Dad told us. She died of a stroke. I guess all of them. The four and the undertaker put him in the casket. If I knew about david I would never have sold this house to you. But neither of us got married. Dad just said it was a support structure for the house. As big as this house is, no one would have known unless they removed those boards. Mr. Longtree, tomorrow call the police. It will be in all the papers. So do you mind if I stay here for the night? One last time for old time's sake."

"Sure. Sally will put you in the guest room. He, sorry, David looks so peaceful, like he's asleep. Have you ever heard anything or seen anything?

"Oh sure. The door comes open when it's locked. Same goes for the bedrooms."

"All the bedrooms?"

"Oh yeah."

"Dad would say it was a large house, very heavy. It's just taking a rest. Then he would just smile. Then it's settled. Tomorrow we'll call the police. I know a city police officer. He will know what to do."

The next morning. Lewis called Jimmy. "Jimmy, I've got a story to tell. Can you get your captain to let you come out to the house? It may also be in your jurisdiction because of the time of the crime if there was a crime committed."

"Hold on, I'll ask the captain. Be right back."

Within five minutes, Lewis said, "I'll be over in an hour or so. Do you need anything else?"

"Maybe you should bring the captain or someone in the medical examiner's office with you."

"OK. It may take a little longer. What should they bring?"

"Well, tell them it's a one-hundred-year-old body we found in the attic. But keep it just between you and who you bring. Until you both see, you will, I think, understand once you see all the evidence."

"OK."

In about two hours, Jimmy and Fayette, one of the assistant medical examiners, pulled up in front of the house.

"Wow! I never have known this place was over here."

"Oh! Girl, you haven't seen anything yet. Wait till you see inside."

"Are these people rich?"

"Well, yes and no. Just got a deal on the house all furnished. Just TLC was all they needed. They are nice people."

"You're not going to ring the bell?"

"No, he said just come on in."

"Wow!"

"Is that all you got to say?"

"No. Wow! Wow! I've only seen houses like this on TV or in movies. It's big. Solid stone eighteen inches thick. Even those pillars out on the porch are stone."

"Hey, Lewis, how's it been?"

"Fine until now. No more ghost."

"Oh that."

"What are you talking about, ghost?"

"Oh at the Christmas party, his son and a friend said they heard ghosts in the attic. Boy, were they scared. Jimmy, you might be scared of ghosts after today."

"Oh, I'm sorry, Lewis, this is Fayette Jones. She's the medical examiner."

"Glad to meet you, Fayette. Everyone is in the kitchen, kids are at school. The kids, they know what's going on, everyone."

"This is Officer Jimmy Hines and the medical examiner Fayette Jones. Just introduce each other and please sit. Let's get started. Sally has some lunch for all. Afterward, you two are the only ones that don't know. So let me speak. Just listen, then you can ask questions, and you will have plenty."

Lewis started telling the story to all again. When he finished, he asked if there were any questions.

"Yes. You say this David has been in the attic for one hundred years in a casket. He looks as if he died yesterday. And he had elephant disease."

"Here is the diary of Thomas Carver. Both of you read it. At the time of David's death, it was the police from the capital that would have jurisdiction over this area at the time in 1901."

"Yes, then they would have, would they still have it even today?"

"I don't think so. Today they might have to shine with the county or even with the state. Let me ask before we go up there. Do you think the kids heard the spirit of David up there and these other noises?

"I don't know."

"Tim, you knew nothing?"

"If I did, I would still own this house. I would have paid someone to remove the body and bury it in the family plot. Then I would have sold the house. So far, the only crime was to notify a doctor or the undertaker. So paperwork can be filled out. Back then, it was different than now. Then when someone died, if he or she was in very good health or very young, he or she would have been turned over to a doctor. Remember, doctors were different then. As were the undertakers. They are called funeral directors now. And half of the doctors were not even doctors. They sold snake medicine. So what do you say we take a trip up to the attic and back in time? Follow me."

They arrived in the attic. "Wow! Look at the walls. They are beautiful. And this, David did all this?"

"Yes. Here is what we call the square. We've been in. You two go in first and see for yourself." When the two entered and saw David, their mouths just dropped, and they didn't say a word. They just stared.

"I studied elephant diseases and other rare form of diseases but never one this close up. And to be over one hundred years old?"—

"Dr. Jones, you can touch David. He's firm. He just feels of hard leather."

"Let me get my bags and some things out of the car. By the way, once this is over, it's going to be in the news. Every newspaper and news channel, it will be headlines."

Tim just said, "So be it. I guess since David is my uncle, he belongs to me. But, Lewis, you found him. I would like the whole world see him as he is now. His work up here in the attic and all his paintings and drawings. To be seen. I never knew him, except maybe his spirit floating, so to speak, in this house, trying to contact us and telling us where to find him. David, you're my great uncle, we've never met, but I'm going to honor you. I would have loved to see you when you painted these walls. I read a letter addressed to you from your father. It was placed in your casket after you died, and he wrote it, with your permission. And if Lewis will help, it will be read when we will have services for you in the church, and the letter will be buried with you. You will be laid to rest between your father and mother."

"I'm back. Why don't all of you go have some coffee?"

"It may take some time. Jimmy, you stay with me and help. He's big and probably still heavy. Let's go, folks, Sally will have some lunch."

"Here, I made some fresh coffee and some soup. This will do. I've got a ham in the oven. We'll all still be here for dinner."

"Mr. Longtree, I never asked. What about yours and Sally's parents. Where are they?"

"Our parents passed away before we were married. My parents were missionaries. They were in the South Pacific. On Borneo in that area. I was born there. I was ten years old when they came back home. Taught the Bible at a college that was run by the church they belonged to. I went to public school here. Then in college I was going to be a missionary same as them. But I like to draw, so I became an architect. But my faith, you might say, has rubbed off unto me from Mom and Dad. With I was brought up, it's what's inside that counts. On Borneo, I saw some unusual things. It's like this house we lived in, a condo, two bedrooms, and one bath. We wanted to save enough to buy a house that would last us until we're gone and we could pass it on to the kids. We look in the capital for some very nice and large places. Then we just came out here one Saturday. We saw this house and a sign saying "Up for Auction." We got as much info as we could, and when the final price came down and said sold, I almost passed out. I paid more than twice what it was appraised at. Way, way over our budget. Some people would say karma. I would say someone up there." He pointed with his index finger, meaning toward God. "Guess he wanted us to have it. My parents were born on Borneo. They were raised side by side. Both parents belong to the same church and taught school and the Word of God. They got killed in a head-on collision. The other driver was also killed. He was driving on the wrong side of the freeway. They wanted to be buried in Borneo, so that's where they are. We're going to visit them and help build a clinic. We'll be gone from July through September. Sally will bring the kids back for school."

"Sally, what about yours?"

"Mom and Dad were teachers. Dad was a coach in football in upstate New York. He had a stroke while a game was being played.

He died before they got him to the hospital. Mom, at the time, had cancer, and Dad's death didn't help. So I stayed in town instead of going to college. Then almost two years later, Mom died. I sold the house to pay the medical bills and went to school. I was working part-time at a bookstore. That's when we met. Lewis came in looking for certain books. He was different, a perfect gentleman. He said 'yes ma'am, no ma'am.' He made an impression, and I asked if he was part Native American [you know, Indian]. He smiles, said yes, and asked why. I just said Longtree. He smiled and said, 'If you want to hear how that name came into play. Have lunch with me.' I said yes."

"Oh, by the way, Lewis, where did the name Longtree come from?" They all laughed.

"Well, anyway, this house with all the furniture and everything else is worth some money. The sale of the colonial pieces, I had them appraised. They brought more than three times the appraisal, enough to pay the house off, give back to the town, and more even after taxes are paid."

"And what about the attic?"

"Well, like I said, once this business is taken care of, we'll talk it over, and I think David might approve. We're going to take pictures of everything, yes, even David. And twice a year, the house will be open to all to show David's work, and yes, we will have his pictures to show what he look like. It may bring hope to others like David or to anyone that may look different than the general population. We'll charge a fee and have some of his paintings and those on the wall of the attic taken and reprinted, signed by us. And numbered once sold. And all 100 percent of the fees and sales will go to a fund. We decided to call it the David Carver Memorial Fund. The fund will go toward research for the elephant disease. I think David and yes, his parents, would approve of it. Well, here they come. I'm going to have to turn this over to the state. But for one, it's been over one hundred years and no one to arrest. Two, from my findings, there was no foul play. His tumor was pressing on his brain so heavy before he died. Made him, yes as some would say, he went mad. Then he had another large one pressing on his lungs and heart. He just gave out before he died and could not move. The only thing I could find, nothing but natural cause. Back then, lots of people died at home, and the undertaker would come, and lots of times they didn't remove the body. They brought the casket to the house, put the person in it, and if it was cold outside, they put him in a barn or some type of outhouse to keep him from smelling. Then they would bring him inside for a wake, then church, then the cemetery. I will have to file this. I took pictures of David and the entire square and the attic itself. I'll make sure you folks will receive copies of everything. One more thing. Be prepared for this town to be flooded with reporters and TV crews until David is laid to rest. It will be headlines."

By the next afternoon, the city, county, and state police were in town; and the newspeople followed. The house was full, and Eddie kept the news reporters off the property. It took all afternoon and up until midnight before all was settled. There was no foul play. The only crime was that they buried the body, so to speak, in the attic without a permit. So it was left up to Tim since David was his uncle. Before Tim left, he signed a letter leaving everything to the Longtrees. David was theirs now, and they could do with him as they saw fit. Then Tim said good-bye to David and Eddie, got in his car, and drove off.

"Well, everybody is gone, even the reporters. What are we going to do?"

"We, the family and I, believe the town will agree. We'll have a proper service for David. Nobody knew him, but he was a part of this town, just look at the more is on the attic wall. Thomas loved his son, but yet he was ashamed of him or himself, thinking he had done wrong and God took it out on David. His writings, it could go either way. That's why he had large doors and wide hallways and stairs. He was free to roam the house after six at night and maybe even outside and back to his cell by eight in the morning. The reporters will be back tomorrow. Maybe by then we'll know what to do. But for now, it's almost one. Let's get some sleep. I called in. They know I'm not coming in."

That night, Fearless jumped off the bed and went and stood at the attic door. He was not growling, just staring. Then Missy appeared from Shirley's room and sat beside Fearless. Both were staring up at the closed door. The next morning, all were at the kitchen, when lo and behold, reporters were all over the front porch. Lewis opened the door and he heard so many words. He said, "We have nothing to say at this time. When we do, you will be notified. Now please, leave this property. And show some respect. Thank you."

But to his surprise, they left and went to the small diner. George, the owner of the diner, was having a field day. More customers today than he's had all week.

"Kids, Eddie is going to take you to school and pick you up. Do not say anything to no one, no matter who asks."

"OK. We won't say anything."

Shirley said, "Me neither."

"Fine, see you later. Eddie is waiting for you. Go out the back way."

"Well, what have you decided?"

"I think we should have a church service and take these oil and drawings and place them around and let the people see what he was really like. Also, I believe we should let the people of this town and the world see David."

"You mean open casket?"

"Yes, why not? Let everyone see a man in pain both inside and out. Yet he can paint these oils. And also, I'm going to read the confession of his father to all. And if God will permit, he just might let David hear it also."

"Lewis, maybe Thomas read it to David before he put it in the casket."

"Yes, he might have, but the people I believe should know. It was heartbreaking for them both. I'll go later and see about having his grave dug up and set a date for the service. It will be a packed house.

"Yes. It will be packed for the first time in a long time."

"You know, Sally, what happened here one hundred years ago. And now, this just might help this town and people everywhere to look at each other in a better light. The reporters are still outside. Well, the kids are still at school. We'll let them come in and give them a tour of the house and, yes, even David. Then we will tell them when the service is. And ask them not to bother us until then."

"Ladies and gentlemen, quiet please, I'm going to do you a favor. My wife and I, while the kids are at school, will give you a tour of the house. And yes, the man who is in the attic. You will see him too. Take pictures, then I'm going to ask you to leave and not come back until we have services for David at the first church. If you agree. If not, the ones that come back on this property will be arrested. You will go to jail. I will keep my promise if you will keep yours. Is it a deal? All agree? Fine. In one hour, be here, you will all stay together, if anyone tries to go upstairs on their own, the tour is off. I will have the county and state police here to keep everything under control. Thanks."

Within the hour, the tour started. Lewis and Sally told them all about the house and who built it. All the furniture was with the house from the beginning, then the oils and drawings. That they were everywhere all signed with a large D. That David Carver died from his illness and that there was no foul play. Lewis and Sally told them to just look at David's paintings and that he stood seven feet tall—very big and heavy. That's why the doors ceilings, hallway, and the stairs were tall and wide. He stayed in the attic during the day.

When the housekeeper and his wife would leave at six sharp, David came downstairs. And after dark, he even went outside. He was in the attic before eight the next morning. Then he got so heavy, he could not climb the stairs. He had a large tumor in his brain and another pressing his heart and lungs.

"Now we'll go upstairs. The door to the attic is at the end of the hall. There are three locks on the door. It was put there for David's protection and, yes, the protection of the family near his end. He was, what they called then, going mad. When he could not walk, the family bathed him and fed him until he died. Mr. Carver went to the capital to an undertaker and paid him well. They brought him back here, and with the help of only the family, prepared him and put him in the same type of casket as his father and mother. The casket was specially made in Italy and stored in New York until it was time and shipped here in a wooden case. The family took it upstairs at night. This is the door, when we go up. There is what we call the square, a large twelve-by-twelve-foot room with one large oak door. That's where he was laid to rest. They nailed large wooden plank boards all over the square and the rest of the walls. When you get up, you will know why. Then you will see the square and, yes, the inside. Do not, I repeat, do not touch anything. You may take pictures of David. He still looks the same as the day he died. Then you will leave. Are we ready? In single line."

When all had entered the attic, all lights were on. Their mouths dropped. Then the cameras were all running and flashes going off.

"This David, he did this?"

"Yes. He could hold brushes, but funny thing, he could not hold a pen to write. That's why he signed his name with the letter D."

It took half an hour. "Is everybody ready to go into the square?"

Lewis then opened the door. As they entered, everything was almost the same. When they saw David, they all began to cry, even the men. No dry eyes were in the house. Then one woman cried out, "How could his father do this to his son?"

"Ma'am, please. When you hear the complete story at the services, you will know the answers."

"I have the most respect for his father, back then one hundred years ago. Think about it. What would you do, put him in a sideshow? If the people at the time would show the respect like we are doing today, David would be the, yes, the talk of the town. People would get to know him and would have loved him. But his father could not take any chances."

"At the service, I will read what he said. Then you make up your own mind."

"Mr. Longtree, will David be open or closed, sir?"

"Open. I believe David would want it that way. There are others out there like him today. You have them on TV. Inside they are human, maybe more so than some of you. Thanks, and the interview is over. Please respect our agreement until the time of the service. Good day to you all."

Within ten minutes, all had left.

"I think that went well, not a dry eye. I think we had better get boxes of tissue. We'll need it."

The service was set for noon. For a town this size, the church was large. The street was lined up from the Carver house all the way down Carver Street. People from everywhere, all came to see one man, David Carver. He died 1901, one hundred years ago. And today, he would be finally laid to rest. Then the casket was brought out of the house. It was eight feet long. All bronze and oak. It took twelve men on each side to carry it. Eddie was in front, and the Longtrees were behind. Fearless and Missy watched from Tony's bedroom window. They put the casket on a flatbed, and slowly, it went toward the church. Every man took his hat off, and some crossed themselves. They saw what David looked like on the news and the masterpieces he created. One woman said he had the soul of the saints inside. Then he was put in front of the altar through the side door. It was used only to bring in caskets for service and taken out the same way.

The townsfolk were invited to sit in the front. Cameramen were everywhere. All would get to view David. No one would be left out. Then when the church organ played and the choir sang, a man came in from the rear up to the casket and placed twelve red roses next to David. It was Tim, crying. Lewis pulled a seat and Tim sat next to his uncle. Then the service began. After the minister gave the opening prayer, Lewis stood before David, Tim, his family, Eddie, and the town to read what Thomas, his father, wrote. All the way through, there was not a dry eye. Even a loudspeaker was outside. Even the kids cried. Then after he read what his father wrote and a few more songs were sung, Tim stood up and said a few words and shook Lewis's hand, saying, "You were the right man for the house." Then Lewis stood and looked at David and said, "Your father wrote this and placed it in your casket. I don't know if he read it or not. I will read it to you, David, praying God will let you hear it.

"The Prayer of a Confessor. Oh my David, my son, my loving son, flesh of my flesh bones of my bones. Never a bad word came out of your mouth. My heart has hardened. Not for you or because of you. But it hardened because God did this to punish me for my sins. Oh why, my God? Why didn't you taken it out on me? But then I saw into your eyes and your soul. The love you have shown. For me and your mother. Through your eyes and your hands, you gave us masterpieces. But God gave us a son. Now I ask God. This mighty God to forgive me. And take you by the hand and walk you to the promised land, then you can smile and see the angels sing and shake the Messiah's hand. And walk in glory by the master's side. Oh, David, my David. Named after the king. Please forgive me, your earthly father. And wait for me and your mother when we cross over to the other side. Then one day, I do not know when, one will come and take you to that place to wait for me to be with me, by my side. Then we will again be as one. In that place called paradise. Oh, David, my sweet, sweet David. As I close the lid and say good-bye, the angels in heaven are singing to God the most high. We have received another. On, David, my sweet David, I will mourn till the day. I pray I will be carried off to that place and be by your side in paradise. Amen."

Everyone in the church and out, even the reporters, cameramen, the entire town cried. Then Lewis and all said the Lord's Prayer. And as the people passed, some placed a flower or a bud in next to David. A few touched his face; others took pictures, but not a dry eye was to be seen. Then at four, Lewis, his family, Eddie, and Tim all privately said good-bye and closed and locked the lid. Then the rawbears carried David out to the flatbed and to the cemetery and was laid to rest between his father and mother.

It's now been almost two years. The Longtrees kept their promise, and the place was opened twice a year. A book with pictures, yes, even of David and his works and copies of his drawings and oils, were sold. All proceeds went to research in David's name. And the town became, yes, a tourist attraction. Everything seemed fine. Then word came. Tim Carver, the last of the Carvers, had died. The services were held in the same church, and on Tim's request, Lewis was asked to preside. Then Tim was laid to rest in the family plot. Tony and Sally, well, they fixed up another room in the house for play. The attic was kept the same; twice a year it was open for the general public to see. As were some other homes in town, Carver Street was busy once again.

Fearless grew to weigh almost eighty pounds. Missy was ten pounds. And yes, where you saw Fearless, you saw Missy. The house is back to normal. Fearless slept at Tony's feet. Missy cuddled with Shirley. While the kids are at school Sally was busy doing her work for the corporation in the capital. While she was working, Fearless and Missy went up to the attic. They removed the door, and it was on display next to the square. As the little ones climbed the stairs, Fearless's hair was standing on end, and Missy was walking between Fearless's legs. And they entered the square and stared at the large chair that David sat in. And they sat staring at the chair as if someone was in it.

And then they heard a faint sound, so faint only they could hear. It was the sound of a child or an adult laughing, coming from the chair. Fearless and Missy got up back out of the square then ran downstairs. Was it David? Has his spirit returned. Guess only time will tell.

MESSAGE FROM BEYOND

A woman, very scared, ran to the ER at the university hospital. She was very upset and asked the nurse at the desk, "I just got a call, they brought my son in. Where is he?"

"Ma'am, please have a seat. I'll find out what's your son's name."

"Peter Yates. I'm Ann, his mother."

"I'll be right back."

Within five minutes, the nurse returned. "Dr. Golden is in charge. I'll take you to him. He will tell you what's wrong."

The nurse and Mrs. Yates entered a small side office next to the ER. "Dr. Golden, Mrs. Yates is here to see you about her son."

"Thank you, Susan. Mrs. Yates, I'm Dr. Golden. Please have a seat. Mrs. Yates, your son was brought in about three hours ago. I'm sorry we didn't notify you any sooner. He was in bad shape. To help stabilize him, we had to sedate him for his own protection. When they brought him in, he was so bad, all I could say at that time he was out of his mind. All that he was saying was 'Dad, Dad, Dad' over and over again, so we gave him a total checkup, including a CAT scan and MRI. Everyone, including myself, thought Peter was on drugs. Possibly meth. But no drugs was found in his system, and there were no signs of needle marks anywhere. So to keep him from hurting himself, we put him in a coma. He's in ICU. Do you know what he meant by him crying out 'Dad' so many times?"

"Where was my son at when all this happened?"

"At the uptown food court where all the students go to eat. Off campus. The other students that were with him said he looked up, and his face turned white like he had seen a ghost. Then he stood up and started to say something. That's when he collapsed and started shaking and sweating heavily and calling his dad's name over and over. That's when they called 911. The medics had to sedate him. He's very strong for his size. That's why we thought he was on meth. Where is your husband, Peter's father?"

"Frank was killed by an intruder fourteen years ago, today to be precise. He was killed about ten at night at our home. Peter was six at the time. Why do you ask?"

"Did Peter see anything? Can you tell me anything that might help?"

"We were a very tight-knit family. Peter is the only child. My parents live about three hours away on the Ohio River, so Frank had to work that Saturday. He told me to take Peter and my sister Vi to visit our parents. Not too often Frank had to work on Saturday. Peter didn't want to go. He wanted to be with his dad. It was the weekend, so Frank took Peter to the office with him. So my sister and I went, we would be back Sunday. Vi is five years older than me, never married, so we did a lot of things together. All that we know is around ten that night, the neighbors heard a shot. They thought at first it was a backfire, then they heard Peter screaming. All he was saying was 'Dad, Dad, Dad' over and over again. They called 911. When they entered the house, they saw Frank and Peter in a small bedroom downstairs that was being used as his office. A door led out to the patio. He was lying facedown all covered in blood. Peter was also covered in blood, screaming 'Dad, Dad' over and over. Bob and Sue, the neighbors, knew our parents' phone number, so they called. All of us came. They took Peter by ambulance to the hospital for a checkup and to clean him up. When we got there, Bob and Sue told us what had happened. They said Peter must have seen the whole thing."

"Well, he hasn't said a word. Probably he's waiting for you."

He was asleep when his mom and Dr. Golden came into the room. As Ann looked at Peter, she turned to Dr. Golden and said, "Peter said nothing. We tried even our minister and the hospital psychiatrist. He was closed lip."

As Ann related to Dr. Golden about that night, they checked everywhere, but nothing was taken. "Frank must have heard him breaking the glass. We had no alarms and lived in a nice area. After the services were over, Frank was smart. He left a will and took out insurance in case something like this would happen. There was enough to pay the house off, Peter's education, and other bills. A small amount was for his twenty-fifth birthday. The police never found the killer. No clues, nothing. Our house was large, so Vi sold houses. So she moved in with us. We all thought it was the right thing to do, even Mom and Dad. After six months, Peter started to get back to himself, playing with the new pup we got him. At dinner, he started to say grace. He never did before, and at the end, he would also say, 'Lord, take care of Dad and tell me what to do.' We never asked him what he meant by 'tell me what to do.' He was only seven years old.

"As he got older, in his room, he had pictures of his grandparents. Frank was an orphan. Frank knew nothing about whom or where he came from. He tried to find out but to no avail. Also, Peter had a single picture of his dad, me, and Vi. Some nights I would peek in, and he would be looking at his dad's picture. Several times, I would see tears running down his cheek. He would look at him and say, 'The day will come. He will get what's coming to him and meet his Maker, I'll see to it, Dad.' Peter was not into sports. He was like his father. He enjoyed watching them. When he graduated from school, he had a 3.0 and enrolled at state. He liked law but didn't want to be no lawyer. He wanted to go into some kind of law enforcement. He talked about the FBI or Secret Service or Homeland Security. So he studied psychology. This is his second year. Truth is, Dr. Golden, Peter has done everything I've asked him to do. Three years ago, Vi passed away. He took care of everything. I was a wreck. Peter is strong in every way."

"Well, from what you have said, something must have clicked. Peter never once said he saw the man. I believe he did, and it's in his subconscious somewhere."

"Do you think he saw the man that killed his father at the food court?"

"He might have, only time will tell. But for now, for the next day or so, he should remain here. We'll bring him out of ICU, but for now, let's see Peter."

Again, as his mom entered the ICU unit, just once in a while, she could see his eyes moving under his closed lids. Mrs. Yates spent the night and then went home. Bob and Sue still lived next door and had lunch ready. They were at the hospital when Ann came out of ICU. Ann told them what happened. When they left, they told Ann lunch would be ready when she got home. On the second day, Peter awoke but still would not say anything about what happened. After a week, Peter was discharged. He told his mom he didn't remember anything, but the way he said it, she knew he wasn't telling all. But she didn't push it. "One day, yes," she said, "he will tell me."

Peter still lived at home. No sense renting, wasting all that money when home was only twenty minutes away. One night, Ann got up to get a drink when she heard Peter moaning in his sleep, so she peeked in. He was having a nightmare. He was saying, "I know you, your ear, now I know who you are." Then he awoke and sat up in bed. He didn't see Ann, so Ann went into the kitchen and wrote down what he said.

The next day, everything seemed fine. He left and went to class. So Ann went to the police and asked to see Detective Rogers. He was the detective on the case fourteen years back. When Detective Rogers saw her, he knew who she was. That was his first murder case. After saying hello, she asked him about the case. He got up and opened a small file and removed a folder and showed it to her.

"Mrs. Yates, there hasn't been one day that I haven't gotten this out and looked through it again. Maybe after fourteen years, something will stand out. So far, I'm sorry to say that as of today, it's still a dead end. How is Peter? Is he doing OK?"

Then Ann told him what happened at the food court and about the nightmare she overheard Peter having.

"Mrs. Yates, that may be something. Let me do some checking, I'll get back to you. Oh, what is Peter doing now?"

"Oh, he's second year at state, hoping to go into law enforcement. That's what he wants."

"You know, Mrs. Yates, have him come and see me. We're having a recruitment class in the spring. I believe I can get him in after he gets his badge. If he so chooses, he can still go back to state and finish school and get his degree. This police force here is good, and it may be a jump start in case he wants to be an agent with the FBI or higher. Talk to him and let me know."

Rogers sat back after Ann left, thinking what she heard Peter say. "I know you, your ear."

He got up and stuck his head in the chief's office. "I got a lead on every old murder case. I'm going to check it out."

Rogers was a guy that didn't care about what he looked like. In uniform, he was perfect. Out of uniform, he blended in the crowd. So about the same time as Peter was at the food court having a burger, sitting at the same table, same seat as Peter, were mostly students. Some were in suits, but after fourteen years what would a killer look like? That evening, Ann told Peter what she did. Although she didn't say anything about what she overheard him say. So she told him what she did and advise him to "Go and see Rogers about the glass for police recruits."

The next day, Peter called Rogers, and they met. Then Peter filled out paperwork to be accepted into the police academy and soon started to train. Nothing was said about his father's death other than it was still an open case. He informed the school and said he would go back to class once he got his badge. Within three months, he started and had Rogers to help him and his determination to get the highest score he could get. For deep in the back of his mind, he knew what happened that night when his father was killed. And yes, later what happened at the food court. The only thing he could not understand was why he collapsed and went mad. He saw his father's killer. His left ear was a cauliflower ear, and his nose was smashed in, like he might have been a boxer. It was him, but where was he now? He knew one thing for sure. Someone or something didn't want him to say anything that day at the food court.

During the months of training, it was hard, but he endured. At graduation, he was third in his class. His mom was proud. When he got his badge, at Detective Rogers's request, he would train Peter on the street. Most in the station knew what happened to Peter's father and that Rogers was the detective in charge of the case. Just maybe Peter will tell his new partner what really happened, and together they could put an end to the case and give the killer what he deserves.

After months on the street, Rogers had Peter over at his house and introduced him to his wife and two kids. Pam, his wife, took the kids to a movie. She knew what was going to happen. After dinner, Pam left with the kids. They sat down on the patio after a few minutes. Rogers pulled out the folder marked "file number 32532, Frank Yates" and handed it to Peter.

"Read it. I'll be back in a few minutes. I want some answers. You and me, we're going to close this case, for it's killing your mother slowly one day at a time."

With tears in his eyes, Peter, for the first time, nodded and opened the folder. Then Rogers returned; they talked. Then Peter, wiping the tears from his eyes, said, "I will tell you all that I know. It was Saturday night. Dad and I went out to eat. When we returned, there were no cars in the driveway, no lights on. We got back about ten. The last thing Dad said to me was, 'Go change your clothes, put on your PJs. I'm going to put these papers in the office, then we will watch TV for a while just you and me.'

"I had just put on my PJs. I heard the shot. I knew it didn't come from the TV. I just started running downstairs, and I went down the hall. That's when I saw this man. He had a muscular build, flat nose, and a cauliflower left ear. I didn't see his right ear. He didn't see me. I was in the hallway, and no lights were on in the back. Dad must have heard the glass break. Like the report said, it looked like there was a fight. He shot Dad, and he was looking real fast for something to take. We never kept money or valuables in the house, so he took off. It happened so fast, all I could do was scream and grab Dad. That's when Bob and Sue from next door arrived. The man went totally blank from my mind. I knew I saw him, but he looked like if you asked and you did back then, I could not describe him, until I saw him at the food court. I started to stand and yell, 'He killed my dad. Call the police.' Instead I saw my dad in front of him. Dad had an aura all about him. That's when I passed out. But right before I did, that man, I swear he saw Dad. Also, he stopped. He was no more than five feet from me. His mouth opened, and he turned white. That's when I stood up and passed out. Then everything came back to me while I was in the hospital, Detective Rogers."

"Peter, call me Matt."

"OK, Matt."

"Do you believe in ghosts? You know, the hereafter, that sort of thing?"

"Yes. Do you?"

"I do. Right after Dad got killed, I had a dream. It was so real. I saw Dad the same as he was at the food court. Aglow, with an aura about him, saying, "Pray to God every day. I'm with the Lord. Pray to him. He will take care of you. And one day, he will tell you what to do. A few nights before I talked to you about the police force, I had a dream. I saw a badge in my hand. It had the same number as the one I have on now. So I know the Lord will take care of me, and when that time comes, he will tell me what to do."

By nine thirty, Pam and the kids were back. Peter said good night. Matt told Pam, "I'm going in early tomorrow and run something to the captain. Just maybe the database will pick something up."

The captain had Peter in his office for a get-to-know-you-better while Rogers told everyone what happened during roll call. "This murder happened fourteen years ago. Now it's part of us. Patrolman Yates was only six at the time. He's now twenty-one. Let's put this case behind us. And Peter and his mom can get on with their lives."

He told every detail that Peter related to him the night before.

"If you see anyone like what Peter described, don't try anything on your own. Call for backup, even if it turns out to be a false alarm."

When Peter arrived, they took to the street.

"Peter, what do you want to happen to the man?"

"For a long, long time, I wanted to kill him with my bare hands. All the way up to the encounter at the food court when what I believed was the image of my dad, now I believe what the saying that's in the Bible, 'render to Caesar that which is Caesar's, render to God that which is God's.' I believe that means he must pay for his crime according to the law. To God that's between him and his

Maker. Matt, why was he at the food court? I don't eat there. I always went home and had lunch with mom and aunt Vi."

"Do you know what he was wearing?"

"Yeah, a light-green shirt and pants."

"Did it have a creamy arm band?"

"Yeah, light yellow on each arm above the elbow."

"That's the uniform of some of the employees at the food court."

Within the hour, twenty plainclothes police officers were in the food court, asking the vendors about the man with the flat nose and cauliflower lower ear. Finally, they hit pay dirt. One vendor told them, "Yeah. That's Ray Charleston. I hired him about a year or so back. He's on time every day, never said anything bad about or to anyone, kept quiet. He goes to the first church on Vine Street every Sunday and Wednesday nights, stays at the YMCA. Told me something happened to him awhile back, changed him, and turned his life around. Said he saw someone he hadn't seen in around fifteen years."

"Where is he now?"

"Oh, he asked for today off. Said he had to do something, something that God wanted him to do. He might be at the church."

"Matt, are we talking about the same guy? Excuse me, but this Ray, does he have a flat nose and a cauliflower ear?"

"Yeah."

"Are you sure? The left ear?"

"Yeah, used to be a boxer. If he's not here, let's go to the church. Officer, what did Ray do?"

Peter turned to the vendor, saying in a hushed voice, "He killed my father fifteen years back."

"Officer, you got the wrong man. Ray would not hurt a fly. He feeds the stray cats in the back all the time."

"If it's not him, then he has a twin."

As they were leaving, the dispatcher called Roger. "You're not going to believe this. That man you're looking for. He just turned himself in. He's in the captain's office. Man, I guess he's got a story to tell."

Peter and Matt arrived at the station. All the talk was about the boxer with the cauliflower ear. As they entered the captain's office, the man was handcuffed and was sitting in a chair with two officers one on each side of him. Without saying one word, the man said, "I'm sorry for what I have put you and your family through. I'm sorry for killing your father."

Before Peter could say anything, Ray said he was on smack, meth, anything he could use to get high. He didn't even know where he was at that night. He knew what he did, but yet he thought it was a dream until he saw Peter's father's picture in the paper. He left town, stayed gone, got clean, and for some reason, he came back. Why? God only knows. It had been fifteen years.

"I was cleaning myself up. That's when I got the job at the food court. Then that day, I know you're not going to believe me, but I saw your father. He appeared out of nowhere in front of me all aglow. It happened so fast. He said, 'You know what you have done. Now when it's time, you must do the right thing.' That's when you got up, and I looked at you. Your father's image, he was behind you with his hands on your shoulders, smiling and repeating the same thing. It happened so fast. I left, and the next thing I knew, I was in the first row at the first church on Vine, crying, praying to God. Asking for forgiveness. And your Father's voice said, 'I forgive you. When that time comes you will know what to do.' So this morning, as I was going to work, a voice, but not your Father's, said, 'Son, it's time.' So I'm here turning myself in. Let the courts of law do with me as it permits. I feel better, for now I know God is on my side as he had been on your side all along."

The headlines in the paper and on the news said, "Man Turns Himself in for a Murder Fifteen Years Back." The man said that's what God told him to do. Now it's been five years since that day. The trial was over. Even Peter took the stand, asking for mercy for Ray Charleston, just saying it was the right thing to do. Now Peter has gotten a promotion and went back and finished school. He still lives at home with his mom. A burden was lifted from them both. Once a month, they go to a Southern Ohio penitentiary and visit the man that killed her husband and her son's father, for they know he's a changed man. Neither Ray nor Peter have seen any more visions, so to speak. Driving back, he looked at his mom, smiled, and saw the new look on her face. For he knew now that one day, when that day comes, they both, along with Ray, will cross that bridge and go to the other side in paradise.

In God's eyes and in his way, all is forgiven. All sins, if we truly believe, all sins but one, that's against the Holy Spirit.

THE BLACK DOCTOR

A man old and bent with age and standing with the aid of a walker was looking down at some graves in a cemetery way outside of town. The cemetery was overgrown with brush and weeds. It was very hard to find. It was a black cemetery and went back many, many years. Way back even before his time. He remembered this place, remembered it well. He was born in 1909 when his family was sharecroppers. He looked down at the markers. It had been over sixty years, sixty years far too long. His last visit was when he buried his mom. His father died when he was fifteen. His mom and the older kids tended the fields. Most went to the owner, the balance hardly enough to keep the family fed. His mind drifted back to that time when he was a small lad. He helped pick cotton. He had no shoes, just worn-out pants that had been cut off to make shorts. It was in that part of the South where the Klan ran amok.

He had seen men, young and old, hanging from trees or shot then dumped in front of their houses because they said the wrong word or talked to someone other than their own. It was a hard life. If you asked, his answer was "I've seen it all." He made a promise to his mom. One day he would take his mom and the rest of the family North to a much safer place and put this life far behind. He worked hard for his age. School? What school? If there was a school, he didn't tend; the town had a dump where his family, like others, would salvage items like broken chairs to beds, clothes, worn-out shoes. And the books and magazines he would find he'd take home. He was self-taught. He read slow at first, one line at a time. He looked at the magazines the townsfolk would get from Atlanta or further North. One day, he would say, he would leave this place far behind, and go to those places and make a name for himself, if it took the rest of his life.

Then one morning, at the beginning of his prime, his mom died. The next day, they buried her next to his dad. With determination, he set a goal. His mom told the kids, "When you get older, leave this place. Leave it far behind." But none would leave, so he set out on his own. He walked, caught rides on the train like hobos, until he crossed that Mason and Dixon line a few times along the way. People would give him work for little pay. He painted a house and barn. He never painted before, and it took him two months. The woman was nice. He stayed in a small room in the barn. She fed him good; he did a great job. The woman was white, a schoolteacher at that. He told her stories where he was from in the South. They took a liking to each other, formed a bond. At night, she helped him with school. Yes, she was mighty kind. Her husband had died, left her very well-off, with no kids. And yes, her cooking was good, the best he ever had.

Then one night, she gave him a test. "Sit here. You got four hours to do it all. Answer these questions, and if you pass, I will tell you what's next."

The test was hard, but he finished on time. Then she sent him to bed, not in the barn, but in the house upstairs in the back. It was for servants at one time long ago. For now, it had been going on two years. He did everything around the house, shopped with her. And yes, ate at the same table with her. The next evening, she smiled. "You passed the test with flying colors. Now what do you want to do next?"

"If I had my way, I'd go to school and become a doctor to help people, those that are in need. That's what I would like to do."

"Adam, you have been here for over two years. So far, you have read everything in the house, including my husband's medical books. For a boy with no schooling when we met, only what you taught yourself, you're the smartest young man I've ever met. My husband and I are childless although we tried many times. You're the closest person I've had since he died. I know you're black, and yes, I'm white, but underneath we're all the same in God's eyes. This is my gift, I hope you accept. I made a few calls. You have to go way up North, but there is a school, a college, to be precise. I will pay your way. Go there, and become that man you want to be."

So with new clothes and money she gave him, he got on the train heading north for college. He made her a promise. "I'll come back with that diploma in my hand." They hugged each other tight for the first time. To them both, it seemed all right. Time passed. The year 1939, he made it. Four years of college instead of eight. Then he went on to medical school. Then rumors of war were not far behind. When he returned, stepping off the train, there to meet him was his second mom. He made her a promise. In his hand was his diploma, all rolled up. He had crammed eight years of college in four, plus extra time at a medical school. It kept him away except for short visits. He wanted to make his new mom, as he called her now, very proud. His mom now was getting older. As she would say, "I have to lock the doors at night to keep Mr. Death away."

As always, with her help, he opened his office. Most of his clients were black at first; then, as strange as it seemed, the mayor got sick, very sick, and no other doctors were around. He was the only doctor, a black doctor at that. He was called in. He saved the mayor that day. That was only the start. In an old abandoned schoolhouse vacant for many years, with the help of his mom, they both set out to forge new ground. Then the war started. He knew he would be called. Then he was called, so everything was put on hold. They tried, even the mayor, to get him exempted from duty. He was a doctor, and they needed doctors. He told his mom, "Lock those doors. I need you more than Mr. Death."

She made him a promise. "When you get back, that school will be a hospital, with you in charge."

It was 1942 when he got called and went to Hawaii. For a black doctor, to some that broke all rules, but he was one of the best, so things went fine. The war was tragic. He worked on them all, from burns, broken legs, to no legs at all. Then the war ended. He smiled as he got off the train. His mom was there to meet him with some help. Also the mayor, the whole town. He was their hero; his name got in the news, but to his mom, he came back as he promised. After they hugged and embraced, to both it had been a long time. The town had grown a little since he had been gone. Then the parade pulled up in front of the school. It looked different; additions were added.

His mom smiled. "I told you I would fix it up. I believe it's everything you need."

As the years passed, the hospital grew with more doctors and nurses. It was still small compared to some. The word spread that the services were the best and that the name of the hospital was the Sarah Chapman/Adam Warren Chapman Memorial. He took her last name, for it was something he wanted to do. He sent money to his kin. Then, as in all families, one by one they died or just drifted away. He tried to find them but to no avail. One day, he returned home. She had lunch ready. His room was any room of the house after lunch. She told him, "Adam, tomorrow all this will be yours."

"You, my dear lady, you have a long way to go."

"Adam, remember, I told you I locked those doors at night to keep Mr. Death away. I think he has the keys."

Then, without asking, he took her in for a checkup. She smiled. "I'm ninety-nine. Are you sure you can find my veins and heart?"

"Oh yes, your heart, it runs all the way through you." After all the tests, he told her she was fine. A few months later, the town gave her a birthday party. She was now one hundred. A few days later, they had friends over for dinner. Afterward, she went to bed while Adam and the rest were in the parlor. They saw a bright light at the head of the stairs. They tried to go up but were stopped dead in their tracks. The warmth of the light went through them all. Then they knew. It wasn't the angel or Mr. Death, but God's Son. He came to take his mom to a better place. They say it's on the other side.

When they went in, she was sitting up in bed with an old Bible in her hand. Her fingers were pointing to John 3:16. He buried her next to her husband. When the will was read, she left everything to her son, her only son, Adam. She left it all. Now it has been many, many years since that day. He'd retired but was still in charge. He never found his siblings, never got married, worked most of the time. Now he looked at the markers, just cheap stone slabs. Then he heard the rumble of trucks. Yes, they were on time. In little over three months, the cemetery, it was all restored, with a high iron fence all around. To those that were buried there, he had their names put on new gravel stones. The old ones were placed in a small chapel he had built with pictures of what happened there and the area in the past. Now he was back looking at their graves one last time.

"Yes," he told them both, "it's been a long, long time. This place will be kept and maintained. I've set up a fund to make it so, for my home is far away. But one day, I don't know when, I'll join you both and my other mom in that place. It's called many names. I know where it's at. When that time comes, I'll go into the light and be with the Lord and with all of you in paradise that's on the other side."

NURSE JODY

A young girl, only sixteen, entered the ER room at a hospital. She was bleeding very bad. As she tried to speak to the nurse in charge, she fell down. That was when the nurse noticed that the young girl was in labor and bleeding. As the nurses then the doctors worked on the young girl, all she gave was her name, Mary Morgan. They told her that she was due, but they would have to perform a C-section. When it was all over, the young girl had lost a lot of blood, but in return she bore twins—a boy and a girl both in perfect health. They brought the twins and placed them next to her. She was weak. Then the nurse asked her, besides her name, who the father was and where her parents were. She told the nurse she didn't know her parents. She was placed in foster care at age four, was abused by them, and at the age of fourteen she ran away. She stayed on the streets doing anything to stay alive. She didn't do drugs. Mostly she shoplifted then resold the items on the street. Then she met this young man. He said his name was Matt, no last name. On the street, no last name was used. And if they did tell their last name, it was made up. Then she found out she was pregnant and told Matt it was his. That was the last time she saw him. No one in the area she was from ever saw him again. Then she got worse. After three days, Mary died.

The hospital did a checkup and background check on Mary. She told the truth. She was taken from her parents at age four. Her father was an alcoholic who beat up his wife all the time. So they took her and placed her in foster care for a short time. Her father got into a bar fight; then he was stabbed and later died. Her mother gave the girl, Mary, up, for she was young herself. The system tried to get her adopted, but most wanted a baby. So she was sent to foster homes. All the foster homes were the same. They abused her in one way or another. She told the nurse the reason she ran away was because her last foster parent, he came to her room while his wife was away, and raped her. He told her he would kill her if she ever told. He would do this every time his wife went out. Until one night, when all was asleep, she walked out and never returned. She wanted to go to the police, but his threat made her run very far.

All that happened in New York. She was in Philadelphia now. The nurse felt sorry for Mary. He told her before she died, "I'll do my best to find your mother. Maybe she has changed and would welcome you back home."

During the weeks after Mary's death, the nurse managed to contact Mary's mother. She had remarried and had two kids and a nice husband who lived in Boston. Mary's mother told the nurse that her husband and her kids didn't know about Mary or about her first husband and wanted it to stay that way. She said, "Give the babies up for adoption just like I did. If you contact me again, I'll sue you."

That was the end of the line for the nurse. Jody, the nurse, knew the babies would be separated. Not very many people wanted twins. So she did one thing before they took Mary away. She clipped two pieces of fingernails and two locks of hair and bought two lockets and put the nail and lock of hair behind the picture of Mary, a picture she took. Nurse Jody knew that if she did this and they were separated, one day they might meet and put two and two together. Jody was forty when all this happened, but something drove Jody to do what she did. One more thing, she would keep an eye on the twins even after they were adopted. within two weeks. They were adopted by different parents. The agency that was in charge gave the parents the lockets, saying they belonged to the baby's birth mother. Most parents don't tell their kids if they were adopted, and a lot do.

Jody did what she said she would do, watch them from afar. Why she did, she didn't know. But Jody did one more thing. She contacted the New York police and told them what happened, so the police and children services went backward to when Mary ran away. And the records showed the couple was still doing foster care after checking their records. All they took care of was girls, no boys. Then they interviewed those girls. Some were young women now, but they were still afraid to tell. Then one got up the nerve, and the rest followed. They arrested the man and charged him with seven rapes to minors under sixteen. His wife didn't know. Jody had to go to court. They asked her why she did this. All she could say was something inside said it was the right thing to do. And for Mary, if she wasn't raped, she might have lived a good life and got married; but that man destroyed her life and the lives of the other girls. He got twenty to life on each count.

Now Jody was still working as a nurse. She was sixty now. The two twins, they were twenty and fine. Within six or seven years, she would retire, or that's what she said. She kept her word. She had never done this before or since even at the first sight of Mary. Theirs was a bond. A bond strong as kin. During those twenty years, Jody watched from afar, and as she watched them grow, something the two would do, if they were put together, you knew they were twins. They were named Joseph and Rachel, and all these years they never met or ran into each other. Now at twenty, they were off to school. Joseph was studying law. He was very bright and could speak three other languages—Mandarin, Spanish, and French. He wanted to be a diplomat, so he studied international law.

Rachel was studying to be a doctor. She wanted to work with the underprivileged, to help them out. They both went to the same school. During their years at college, Jody could not keep an eye on them like she wanted. So she thought they would be all right. Then one evening, Jody was going through some old papers in the trunk. She was sixty and was never married. Then she came upon a piece of brown paper. As she opened it up, her mouth open and tears came into her eyes. Then she sat down and remembered back when she was so young. She had almost forgotten. Was this why she watched over those twins all these years from afar? Then she folded the paper and went to the hospital. It was her day off. No one in records paid any attention. They knew her; she was in records at least twice a week for one thing or another. She searched. It took her all day. After phone call after phone call, she found what she was looking for.

And tears started to run down her cheek. Now Nurse Jody, she didn't, and yet she did know what to do. But how? The next day, she took a dozen yellow roses to Mary's grave, knelt down, began to cry, and prayed. As she cried, she cried out to God. "Now I know why Mary felt so close to me. As if she was my own kin. Oh God, what shall I do?" As she was praying, she felt a hand on her shoulder, saying, "You know what to do. I'll be with you all the way through. For now you know, the young girl Mary is your granddaughter and the twins. That you watch over are your great-grandchildren."

Now Jody, her heart was laden, and yet she felt relieved, saying, "Now I'll start from scratch, for things have to be all right, for God is watching over me. This story, I'm going to leave it where it's at. You fill in the missing links and see if you will come out right."

DEATH ROW

A man was sitting in a small cell and was looking at the clock on the wall. Forty-eight hours to go, forty-eight hours till the state would take him from his cell to a room and would strap him on a table, and then at 9:05 they would pronounce him dead. He was on death row and had been for fifteen years for a crime he said he didn't commit. But to everyone, they were all innocent. As he sat, he looked at the Bible he had read many times. He picked it up, opened it to Matthew chapter five, the Sermon on the Mount, and he started to read and prayed at the same time. He knew he was innocent, but all the evidence pointed to him. As the saying goes, "You're in the wrong place at the wrong time." Then he glanced back to fifteen years past. To a time he wished he could have forgotten he was a young man living in an area infested with drugs.

It was around eleven at night. He was going to a carryout two blocks down to get a pack of smokes. He knew the owners. When he got near the carryout, he heard three gunshots. He knew something was wrong. He ran as fast as he could, turned the corner, and ran into a man wide-eyed and scared to death, with a large scar on his right cheek. He knocked him down. He didn't stop and just kept on going. When Brook got up, he ran to the carryout and went inside. Malcolm, the owner, was on the floor and was shot with a gun. It was next to his side. Without thinking, he picked it up and set it to one side. Then he helped Malcolm. That's when the police arrived. With their guns pulled, they made Brook to get facedown, Malcolm was already dead. They arrested Brook, charged him with murder in the first degree. All the tests showed Brook had residue on his hands from where he held the gun. He tried to tell them what happened, but to no avail. No other fingerprints were on the gun. Plus, there were bloodstains on his shirt.

Also, Brook had a past record. So with a warrant, they checked where he lived. There was nothing, everything was perfectly clean. He told them he didn't do drugs and he didn't drink. He just smoked. He did a year when he was seventeen, he was tried as an adult. He went with a friend to a party where drugs were being used. It was raided, and all were taken in. His friend told the police Brook arranged it all. No drugs were found on him or even in his system. Brook thought it was just a party with beer floating around. He got three years but was out in one. His so-called friend, while he was in, sold drugs to anyone that came along. Then there was a raid, a shoot-out, and his friend was killed. When Brook heard about it, he called his attorney. After much work, the warden said he wished all the inmates were as good as Brook, so he got out and got a job.

But his record still remained. Now it has been ten years, back to court for another crime he didn't commit. During the trial, both sides were heard. Even the brother of Malcolm said Brook didn't do it. The court was full of people on Brook's side, but all the evidence, three bullets, made the people of the city fed up with all the crime committed with guns. To the jury, it was a crime that deserves the same. Now at forty-two, his life—what life, he has had none—he had spent sixteen years total of that life in a cell for two crimes he didn't commit. After reading the Sermon on the Mount, he prayed. Many years before he gave his life over to God and his son. Right after he went to jail the first time, he's never given up hope or faith.

Besides the Sermon on the Mount, the other story he enjoyed reading was of Job and all the troubles he had. But Job never gave up. He kept the faith in God. Then at the end, God restored all that was taken from him. With less than forty-eight hours to go, he prayed, "If this is the way it must be, I have forgiven all. From the judge, the jurors, the police, even the man with the scar."

As he prayed, he opened his eyes. He saw the man, the man with the scar was at a bar, watching the news about the execution that was to occur in less than forty-eight hours. He saw the man's face. To his surprise, tears were running down his cheek. Then the man got up and left. Then Brook was staring into space when a bright light appeared. A voice only he could hear, said, "I am your salvation. I am all that you need."

Brook started to cry and said, "Do with me as you please, for you are my Lord. You shed your blood for me, now I'm ready, for that time has come. I pray you take me with you to paradise."

Then a force like he never felt before brushed against his face. His tears were wiped away, so he smiled and thanked the Lord.

"Now I'm ready. I'm not afraid. I'll be with my Maker in paradise on the other side."

Then he lay down on the bunk and fell asleep. When he awoke, the warden and guards were outside. He looked at them then the clock. He smiled, yet it was not that time. Then the warden spoke. "Brook, the governor called. You got a stay. A man crying ran into the police station and confessed to the crime. He had a scar on his right cheek." Within two weeks, Brook was set free. The man with the scar confessed to it all. He said he was at a bar when he saw Brook on his knees, praying. He ran out and there in the alley was this light. It said, "Your name is Luke, you know what you have done."

Luke said, "I said yes. The voice then told me I must do what's right. It said, 'When that time comes, I'll be with you to the end and beyond. For I am he that was dead but lives, and I live in you. Do you believe?' I said yes and turned myself in."

In court, Brook was cleared of all charges, even the one when he was seventeen. A total clean slate. At the trial of Luke, Brook told the court what Luke saw was true, for he himself saw Luke at the bar, then the light.

Brook said, "Do not condemn Luke to death. For I forgave him many years ago."

Luke pleaded guilty and was given fifty to life with parole in twenty-five. Luke looked at Brook and Malcolm's family, asking for forgiveness, with a bright look on his face. With two guards with him, one on each side, he turned and walked away.

With all those years in prison behind him, Brook now preaches the Word of God. He has his own church. Every Sunday and during the week when services are held, it's standing room only. Now Malcolm's family attends and stands by Brook's side. So once a month, Brook, now Reverend Brook, goes to prison. He sees Luke and holds services for all. When it's over, Luke hugs Brook, for they both know they are special. For they were touched by the spirit of God.

THE TEENS

A young teen was walking down the street and looked into an alley and saw three other teens beating an old man who was lying on his face, unable to get on his feet. The teens kept beating the old man, laughing, and calling him names. They saw the teen and asked if he wanted to join in. The teen went over, but instead of joining in, he pushed the others aside and turned to give the old man a hand. They grabbed the teen and beat him to a pulp. Then, laughing, they left both in the alley alone. They said, "Too bad for them. Yeah, look at them. They both look like they could be dead."

A little while later, someone saw them and called 911. They were rushed to the hospital. Both were so badly beaten. The doctors thought they were dead. After hours of surgery, the old man came to. But the teen was not so lucky. They put him on life support. That was all the doctors could do. His family was found, and they rushed to be by their son. Their only son. Then the parents called their minister, within hours after they were found, news of what happened spread all over town. The old man had just lost his way. The teen was on his way to help his grandparents. He always walked, for they didn't live that far away. The whole neighborhood knew the teen. They say he wouldn't hurt a fly and helped out anyone that was in need. That was how he was raised, and that was what he believed.

The church and everyone prayed for the teen to recover, but at last, his heart stopped. To their faith and their belief, the angels took him away. He had always told his parents that when he died, they should give what's left of him to others so they could live out their lives to the fullest, until that day when they would be taken away.

This story does not end here, for it's only the beginning. God works in mysterious ways that we here will never understand. The three teens who beat the two were from a better part of town, and with nothing else to do, They were driving fast to get far away from the scene. They weren't high on drugs. They had seen scenes like this on TV, a random beating, getting a thrill—a high, so to speak. It was supposed to make you a better and bigger man. But little did they know, destiny was with them that day. In the car, going very fast, they ran a light and hit head-on into a tree. All three were in the front and had no seat belts on. They nearly died at the scene.

As they barely opened their eyes, all that they could see was a young man, a teen, coming to help. They knew this teen. He was the one they beat up along with the old man. How did he get here so fast with no bruises or cuts? As he came to them, there was a smile was on his face.

"Do you know me? Do you know who I am?

They nodded their heads yes.

"Why then did you do it? Why did you beat the old man?"

All the three could say it was for the thrill of the game. Then he told them, "Look at me. Remember me. You killed me, for now I am dead."

Then everything went black. When they came to, they were in the hospital. They were just knocked out. They didn't even have a bruise. When they were fully awake, they heard the news of the old man and the teen. The old man was alive; the teen was dead. They looked at each other, afraid to speak. Then they were told that the teen died at the same time their car hit the tree. Alone at last. They looked at each other, saying, "We must make amends. We have to tell." Who will believe them?

Then the teen appeared before all three, saying, "My body is in the next room, lying on table."

The three started to cry, asking for forgiveness and asking what they should do.

"I forgive you. For God the Father sent his son, that through him we can be forgiven, if only we ask and believe. For that's what I've always believed."

What would you do if this happened to you? Would you believe the teens? Or are you thinking they were doing this to get off with a slap on the wrist? Or in court, would you say, "Give them the third degree" or "Teens, your honor, teens will be teens"? What would you do? The teens walked out of the room, looked down the hall, and seeing the doctors and the police talking to a couple who was crying, they then looked at each other and said, "There's only one thing to do."

They went, and in front of them all, they told their story and what they did. All told the same story. No one believed them. The police took their statements and then took them in. The parents asked the doctor if they could see their son one last time before they took him away. As they held their son's hand and began to pray, the light we have all heard about filled the room. Then their son appeared. He told them, "They told the truth. So forgive them, for they know not what they did. They will live with this for the rest of their lives. For me, I forgive them. For I'll be on the other side in a better place. I will wait for you, when that time comes, on the other side."

The story does not end here. The teens would go to court. The parents who lost their only child, the old man, all would be there except the young teen who tried to help and lost his life. They would be sentenced according to the law, but look into their eyes, the eyes of the parents and the teens. What do you see? Yes, it's hard to believe, for when it was all over, the teens and the parents from all sides hugged and wept together. And somewhere nearby, a teen was smiling. Then something caught them all in the corner of their eyes. The parents saw their son, the teens saw the one they killed, and then he smiled at them all and finally went with someone—and yes, we know who—into the light.

MAN IN THE PARK

It was a beautiful day, not a cloud in the sky. He had the day off, so why not go walking in the park? The park was large and was at the edge of town. Parts of it were mowed, with flowers and shrubs planted all around. Other parts were left for nature to tend. There were joggers, bikers, and families with kids, all enjoying the sunny day and having fun. But it was strange that there was this many people here at the park. In the middle of the week.

He stopped by a vendor, bought a dog and a Coke, and sat down on a bench and began to eat. He sensed something and looked around. That's when he noticed no birds. The park was full of them, all waiting for someone to give them some crumbs or other goodies to eat. It was strange, so he finished his lunch and put the trash in a can next to the bench. Then he walked past the flowers and shrubs toward the woods. That's when he stopped. The birds, now the people, they were all gone. He ran back to the entrance of the park. He must have gone crazy; he must have gone insane. As he looked out, there was no town. He turned around, and there was no park, just lots of trees. Some rolling hills, not a sound he could hear. Nothing, no birds in sight. Even the wind was still. The area that he was in and what he could see was the most beautiful place he had ever seen. The sky was perfect blue, and the land, the trees, even the streams, all were perfect. And nothing, not even a blade of grass, was out of place.

Where was this place? It was so beautiful. How could something like this ever exist? He started walking toward the smell. Where did it come from? Where was it? He could smell all kinds of flowers and trees. Then he saw the flowers, the trees, all in full bloom right before his very eyes. He wondered if this was Eden, the place where Adam and Eve were created. Or was he dreaming all this right from the start? As he walked, he looked down at his feet. He had no shoes, no socks, and he was barefoot. And his clothes, they were gone. All he had on was a long white robe. Everything about him had changed. He looked into a stream, and he saw that he was a young man, not sixty—that was his age before he entered the park. His arm, it was all healed. It was crushed when he was young and working at a mill.

He felt different, all alive and like new. "I must be dreaming this. If I am, I don't want to wake up."

Then he saw a bridge on the other side, people all aglow, standing, smiling at him. The glow shone from them, somewhere from within. He stepped on the bridge and got halfway across. He stopped, and he could go no farther. It was like an invisible wall. Then a light came forward and stopped in front of him. The light was more brilliant than those lights that were emitted by the people on the other side of the bridge.

"Do you know who you are and where you are at?" the light asked.

"I know my name. This place must be Eden or better yet. As beautiful as it is, it must be paradise. Yes, paradise, and I don't want to leave."

"Across the bridge is paradise," said the light. "This side is halfway between your world, the world of man, and my world. You see, my world, it's across the bridge, but you can't cross. For it's not your time. Your time will come."

He said, "I hear that voice. It's the most beautiful I've ever heard. I know it's coming from the light. I can't see you—"

Before he could finish, the voice said, "Only those on the other side can see who I am. Do you know who I am?"

The man started crying. "Yes, I know. You died on the cross for me. I believe. Why can't I go across and see you in paradise?"

"Speak my name."

"You're Jesus, the Son of God."

"Then I will tell you, for it's not your time. You do not remember. I will send you back to see. When you return, I will tell you why you can't cross to the other side."

In a flash, he was back at the bench, eating his dog and sipping his Coke. When finished, he put the trash in the can. Part of the bun he gave to the birds like he had always done. He walked past the flowers and shrubs toward the woods. He heard a cry, a cry for help. At the edge of the woods, he saw a man attacking a woman. At his age, he ran as fast as he could. As he ran, something flashed before his eyes. He saw his life before him, from the time he was born, to a boy, a teen, then a young man working at a mill. He remembered it well. He couldn't shake it from his mind. An explosion, men were trapped. He pulled all the men to safety without thinking of his own life. After it was over, that's when he noticed his left arm was crushed. Even carrying the men to safety, he didn't notice. It didn't hurt. He spent weeks in the hospital and later at home. His arm was still intact but of no use. Now he had to start from scratch, to use his right to do the job now for both.

He was a hero to the company and the town. So now he worked in the office. He never told anyone that at that moment at the mill, running to rescue the men, he prayed to God and ask him to help. That's when he saw the light, that same light at the bridge. He gave his life over to God that day at the mill. Now he was doing the same, praying to save someone he didn't even know. When he arrived, the other saw him, aimed a gun and shot him, then ran into the woods. He saved the woman that day and, yes, at the expense of his own. Before he closed his eyes, he remembered those words. What greater gift to give to lay down your life for another?

When he opened his eyes, he was in bed, dressed in a white gown, unable to speak or move, with doctors all around. Then again he closed his eyes. Then he saw that light more brighter than before.

"I have been with you from the time of your birth. You have loved me and accepted me from the time you saw me at the mill. When that time comes, and only my Father knows, you will meet me and see me on the other side of the bridge. I am sending you back. Enjoy your life. Tell others what you saw. Some will laugh and shake their heads, but others will believe."

When he awoke he was lying in bed. He told the doctors what happened and what he saw and asked about the woman. Was she all right? She was fine. They caught the man. Then the doctors smiled and said, "We believe in miracles too. For look at your arm. When you were shot, something happened. We removed the bullet, for it went very deep. We don't know what happened. Now raise your arm, your left."

For the first time in forty years, he could raise his arm without help. He raised it above his head. It had been weeks now. Word of what happened, it was in the past. Now the man, yes, and the woman he saved, that will last for the rest of their lives. Now as he walked in the park toward the woods, one day, instead of these woods, he will see that bridge, cross it, and see the man who died for him face-to-face.

OLD WOMAN AND THE TOWN

A man so rich, so the story goes, came to town and offered to buy it, the entire town. Everybody laughed at him when he made the offer. The offer was for everyone to sell. They all had to say yes; no one could say no. Then they all agreed. All but one old lady, and they called her a fool. They offered her more money if she would change her mind. Then she told them the story of the beginning of the town. It was her great-great-grandfather who came over in a boat, with only pennies in his pocket and the clothes that he wore. After weeks looking for work, he got a job making a dollar a day. He slept wherever he could, for he could not afford a roof over his head. So he saved his money. Still he gave some to people that were poorer than himself. Back then, if you were good with your hands, you got very good pay. He saved his money and struck out on his own. He was good at the work he did, building nice and fancy homes. Then he got an offer so big he could not refuse. He built a mansion. It covered an entire city block. He got paid a lot. He hired people that were skilled laborers but out of work and living on the street.

Then the jobs dried up, and there was no work to be had. His helpers were let go. He was back on the street like before, so he left the city and went from town to town and showed clients drawings of the work he had done. Then a stranger from afar saw his drawings and offered him a job. He took him to a valley. This valley, to be precise.

The stranger said, "Build me a town. You must build it right."

The client had the town all drawn out, homes and shops all around a town square.

"Build this town. Bring in whoever you want. I will pay you fair and square. The first building you must build in the center of the town is a church. This church, then, it will be given to the people of the town."

The church sat on a very large lot in a park-like setting, so he built the town, hiring the people and their families from the city, ones that he knew and had worked for him before. When the town was finished, the man took the old lady's great-great-grandfather to one side.

"Now you and your workers, their families, this town is yours. Move in. I give it to you and the workers, all your descendants." Then he said, "All this is yours. When that time comes, it will happen to you all. You will be buried in the churchyard. There are two more things you must never do. Never sell this town, and this church must never be altered or tored down. For if you do, you will all be fools."

Throughout the years, the town prospered while other towns bit the dust. Her ancestor got married in the church, same as the people that built the town. Their children's children did the same. Then one day, her ancestor passed away. They buried him in the churchyard. Afterward, everyone in town that died were buried there. They liked it that way. About every twenty-five years or so, someone comes in and offers to buy the town.

The old woman said, "We have prospered in this town and this valley for more than 150 years. Now you want to sell? Leave the valley. Go another way."

But the townsfolk were bullheaded. They could only see it their way now. The woman, up in her years, knew she had little time left.

Then she would be buried in the churchyard as the rest. With new people moving in, old ways had started saying good-bye. Then another will come to town and make the same offer to the new residents.

Then the man arrived. All the folks in town were at the church. He asked them, "Have you changed your mind?"

"We're still talking to the old lady. Maybe if you come inside, she may change her mind." He refused, saying the church was old. But he kept saying to himself that it would be the first building to be torn down.

Now the old woman, bent with age, said to the folks, "I've told you before, the town cannot be sold."

The buyer laughed, saying anything could be bought for the right price, even your soul. Then the folks saw who he really was. The sun came out, and he cast no shadow at all. They told him to go and be gone in the name of God. As he faded, he said these words, "I'll be back when you folks have all gone. Then I will tear this secret place down and destroy it, along with the town." Then he was gone.

The old woman whose forefathers had built the town, looked at the people and said, "When my ancestor had built the town, he never knew who the man was or where he came from. They did not receive any money for their labor. They just received the town, free and clear, except for two things. The town cannot be sold as a whole, and the church cannot be altered in any way or torn down. Now let's go inside. Pray to God for him to keep this town alive."

But in time, the old woman and her story might fade away. It's a story, one of many you have heard, but is it true? Only time will tell. New generations, how easy it is to forget. Then one day, another comes and offers to buy the town. Will there be someone there that will remember, or will they all sell, and will they become fools? As the story goes, only time will tell.

TEEN WITH A GUN

A man opens his antique store around eleven every day, trying to make a living to help pay the bills and to keep the wolves away. His shop on the main street of town puts items in the front yard to draw customers inside. Then one morning, after he opened, a young man came in, wanting to sell an old antique lamp. The man looked at the lamp. He noticed a price tag from another shop, and by looking at the man, he knew this lamp was hot.

"I don't buy items like this, but if it works, I have a friend who would buy it. Now how much do you want?" Fifty was the reply. So he called his friend but hit 911 instead. He pretended to talk to his friend, and the operator took the hint and dispatched the police. Then the operator asked if he had a gun. Before he could answer, the man figured out what was going on and started to run. When he got to the door, the police was outside, so he stepped back. Then he closed the door, pulled out a gun.

"Why did you call the police?"

He answered, "I don't buy stolen items, and I saw your gun. It was bulging under your shirt. That's why. Do you know what's going to happen if you go outside with that gun in your hand? They will probably shoot you, shoot you dead."

The young man pointed the gun at his head. "I should shoot you for what you did."

"Yes, if you shoot me, the police will hear the shot and storm in. Then, by all accounts, there will be two dead. You kill me, they kill you. If they take you alive, after the trial, they will put a needle in your arm. Then you will be dead. So why not lay the gun down? I'll walk outside with you, and your parents won't have to bury their son."

Before he could finish, the man said his father was dead, his mother was an addict. His parents, he had none. He said his father was killed selling drugs, and his father got his mother hooked on them. Then when he was born, he had lived in a drug environment all his life. He hated drugs, he had no good education, and he had no record. He was just trying to get by. Yes, he stole the lamp.

Then the man saw a tear in the young man's eye.

"What's your name? My name is Mark."

"My name is Willy. Why do you want to know?"

"You know, Willy, the Good Book says stealing and killing is a sin. Do you believe in God? Have you ever read the Bible?"

"I've never been to church. Why should I? All they do is preach a bunch of lies."

"Here, Willy, I'll show you." He points to a Bible on the desk. It was large, and it was in two parts, the old and the new.

"When you read it and read it right, those words they come alive."

This went on for a couple of hours. The police called and asked for all to come out, but yet there was something in this young man, something good. And yet Mark could not figure it out. He looked at Willy and said, "Do yourself a favor. Touch the book, open it. It's divided into two parts. Most is the Old Testament, the last is called the New Testament. The old is history before the birth of Jesus. The new is based on Jesus's sayings and what he did that changed the course of history and man too. Open it to any part, we'll read it together. Let's see what it says."

Willy opened it and pointed to Matthew chapter 5 and as he read, it was the Sermon on the Mount. After he read it, he asked, "Is this true?"

"The Bible says it is, and yes, I believe it to be so."

Then something happened to Willy. He stared past Mark and asked, "What's that bright light that I see?"

Mark looked around but could not see it. Then the teen heard a voice, a man's voice. It was his father's speaking to him from the light. "I'm your father, you're my son. I did things when I was alive, bad things to you, to your mom, even to my mom and dad. I sold drugs and all those other things that you know about, even making your mom an addict. Back then, I didn't care. When I got shot and before I died, I saw this light, the same light that you see now. As I lay dying, I prayed to God to forgive me for what I have done and to keep you and your mom safe from people like me. Then I heard a voice. It said, 'I hear you and know your name. You are finally speaking the truth. Now call me by my name.' I called his name, Jesus, and asked him to forgive me for what I have done. He said, 'Yes, I will. And now you are mine.' That's when I died. I'm now on the other side. He keeps his promise. I don't have that much time. Go turn yourself in. Remember, God, through his son, will be with you all the time if you believe."

Then Willy laid down his gun and began to cry.

"You didn't see the light?"

"No, Willy, the light was meant for you. Though I didn't see the light, I heard what your father said. The choice now, Willy, is up to you."

Mark held him. He cried so hard that he released all the anger from all those years he had built up inside. When he stopped, he said, "I'm ready. Will you be by my side?"

In court, Willy told what happened, no details, just that he was a confused young man. Mark told the judge, "If you don't send him away, I'll help him the best I can."

Willy got probation, started going back to school. In his pack with the other books, he carries a small Bible that he reads a lot. He got his mother in rehab, and she's doing extremely well.

Mark asked him what he wanted to do with his life after school. Willy looked and smiled. "Mark, you know what I'm going to do. I'm going to preach the good news, the Word of God."

Now as Mark sat in the shop, looking back to that day, he wished and prayed that he had seen the light, that light that he knows was from God. Then he smiled. Yes, he heard the voice, and yes, he still believes that one day, whenever that day comes, he will see and go into the light. Then he too will be on the other side.

MICHAEL

As he awakens and sits up in bed, he stares out the open window, bright and sunny, as a light breeze comes through off the bay. He gets up, takes a shower, dresses, and instead of the usual coffee and toast, he decides to go to Monk's Diner two streets over for some good home-cooked breakfast.

He's thirty-two, five feet nine, of medium build. He was a cop walking the beat until a few years ago there was an accident, an explosion at a meth lab. Singed his right eye, it was now harder to see. His left was OK. Still a cop, but not on the beat; he also carries no gun. Reaching the diner, Monk, the owner and cook, says hi.

"The usual?"

Pete nods and goes and helps himself to a strong cup of joe. The diner was different. Just Monk and his wife, it was almost like home. You helped yourself, and the prices were cheap compared to others closer to downtown. The paper was always free. The rule was that after you read it, you folded it up and replaced it back on the rack.

He was on vacation, so to speak, worked all the time. Took no sick leave, so his time off with the two weeks of standard vacation was almost four weeks. On his regular days off, he would help at the homeless shelter for men when he had the time or at the place where battered women would go to get away from their abusive husbands or the other half. He would talk to them, then pay a visit to those men, show his badge and in so many words, told them, "I don't want to come back. The next time, I'll take you in and lock you up. You know what it's called, that term, the bull pen." When he says that, they know what he means, then he leaves.

He's been doing this for a year now, almost two at the shelter. The men there were different, from all walks of life. Everyone had a different story to tell. Either you believed them or not. Of all the men that he helped, one was a young good-looking man no more than twenty-five. With his looks, he could melt anyone if they looked into those eyes. His name was Michael. He sits and talks to no one, sits in the back of the dining hall. where the men eats. When Pete is there, Michael's eyes follow him wherever he goes.

After breakfast, he talks to Monk then decides to go to the shelter. It's been almost a month. He enters, signs in, everyone says "hi" and "where have you been?" He replies, "Working. No time off."

As he looks around, there in the back sits Michael, staring at him. So Pete decides it's about time that he had a talk with him.

"Hello, Mike, I'm Pete. I help out here whenever I can. Sorry, I haven't said hello before. May I get you a cup of coffee? Something to eat?"

Michael smiles for the first time. "Yes, please. Pete returns with an egg sandwich and two cups of coffee."

"Here we go. May I join you and talk for a bit?"

"Yes, please sit down. You're a cop, aren't you?"

"Yes, I am. I don't walk the beat or carry a gun."

"Your right eye, it's damaged. That's why you don't walk the beat."

"How did you know that? Did someone tell you?"

Then Michael looks out the window, then at Pete.

"If I tell you, you would not believe."

"I've heard a lot of stories from the men here. Most I don't believe, but I'm willing to listen."

"You're thirty-two years old. Live alone at 1221 Baxter Street. Top floor, apartment 32. Your phone number is 5551212. You have been a cop for ten years. Something you have always wanted to do. Not married, never had a girl, dated a few times. You're a loner like me."

"How did you know all this? Have you been stalking me or something?"

"See, Pete, I'm different. I know all about you. When and where you were born, I know all. If you want to know more, we go to your place. It's not that far. There, I will tell you, tell you all. That's if you're ok with it and willing to listen."

They arrived at Pete's place. "Now that we're settled in, I'm listening. Tell me your story I'm all ears."

"First, how old do you think I am?"

"You look around twenty-five, give or take a year."

"Thank you. Now I will tell you what you must know. Why I'm here. My name is Michael. I'm almost as old as time itself. Only the Father and Son are older than me. Now do you know who I am?"

"Michael the archangel? No, I don't believe you."

Then Michael stood up, and his dirty clothes became a long white gown, and a glow from his face made Pete fall off his chair onto the floor. Then Michael changed back to the way he was and sat down.

"Now do you believe?"

"Why me? I'm just a cop, but not a cop. I'm nothing special."

"Yes, Pete. To the Father you're very special. You help out people, you listen, you have never taken anyone to jail. God has a mission for you, and it will take you your lifetime to fulfill."

"Why me? Why not someone else?"

"God the Father and his Son throughout the ages have picked men to do their deed here on earth. He has picked you."

Then Michael, with his finger, touched Pete on his forehead, smiled, and said, "Soon you will know what you must do and use your good judgment that will give you an upper hand."

Then Michael smiled and said, "I must go. There are others like yourself. I must give them a hand. Remember, what you see and don't understand, ask. It will come to you."

Then Michael changed into a bright light and faded away. Pete knew what he saw, that it was real. Then he ate a frozen dinner and, as usual, went off to bed. All that night he had dreams. They were good and bad. Instead of sleeping in, he got up early. Drinking his coffee, he saw before him the diner full of people. The time was one thirty, and the calendar said "11th Today." What was going on? Then the vision he saw were of men wearing masks and carrying guns, entering and robbing the diner, then shooting everyone, eleven total, then they escape in a car. Then the vision faded.

"What should I do?" Then he remembered, "Ask." Then he picked up the phone and called his chief. He told a fib about overhearing three men going to rob Monks at one thirty today. He knew the chief. He was a religious man. If this turned out ok, he would tell him what happened, then maybe he would believe. They both agreed, and around one, the only customers at Monks were cops, dressed in civilian clothes. Then a car pulled up, three men got out, and the driver stayed in the car so they could get away fast. When they entered the diner and started to pull their guns, the cops pulled theirs first. And it ended as fast as it started. All four were arrested and taken away. The chief called Pete over and asked what was going on.

"Sit down," Pete said. "I have a story to tell." When it was over, the chief, with a tear in his eye, said, "I'm glad you stayed on the force. I knew you would do good."

"Then do you believe?"

"Yes, I do. For how else would you know about the robbery at 7:00 a.m.? I know you're in bed even at seven. You don't come in here till nine. Something like this happens again, best you give me a call first."

After filling out paperwork all day, he was told that those robbers had robbed before and were accused of killing twelve people in a string of robberies in the past year. Returning home, he found out that the lights were all on. Seated at the table was Michael, still wearing his dirty street clothes. They looked at each other. Then Michael said, "The job you just did was well done. No killing, for they would have killed them all. Now it's up to your courts to judge them. Then on that day, the Lord will judge them all."

"I have a question, Michael. Is this all, this vision I had, was that my deed?"

"No, Pete, that was your first. As I said before, you're not the only one I have visited in the name of the Lord. You're one of many. Your job, those visions, they are connected to you and the force. You're a cop. When you see these visions, yes, you go to the chief. You, the chief, together you will find away to stop what you see. No blood was shed today. I cannot say about the future, but there will come a time when all men and women will need help, for he will try his best to knock you down, for he knows now who you are. Remember, there is a mystery to God. He and his son has put me in charge of certain things. You are one, so go about your daily life, and when you see these visions, not the dreams, if you need help, ask in the son's name. Then those visions, you may have more than one that's connected, and if you do not yet understand, he will send me to show you. Yet it's up to you how to act on it."

Then as before, he smiled, stood, and faded away. The news of the diner was on TV. They wanted Pete to give an interview, but he declined. The next day, Pete and the chief met at Monks, and he and his wife had a special meal for them. Afterward, the chief went to work, and Pete went to a bookstore. He had never owned a Bible before. So he bought one. On his way back, he was thinking of Michael and wondered, "Does he do this all the time, or does he take a vacation? Nah." Pete knew he doesn't.

So now he knew what his mission was. He still felt the same. His eye did not heal. Even after Michael touched his forehead, and he stopped back at the diner and had a roast beef dinner. Monk again thanked him and asked, "How did you know?"

He looked at Monk and asked, "Do you believe in God? And do you believe he puts into men's hearts this feeling after you have done a good deed?"

Monk smiled. "I've believed in the Father and Son. I wear his cross even though it is under my shirt. But, Pete, you never have spoken of God. You just come in, say hi, read the paper, eat, and leave. Madge and I, we have noticed you in the last two days. You have changed."

Then Pete paid for his dinner, looked at Monk, and said, "The angel of God told me what was going to happen. I acted on it the only way I know now. So God saved us all that day."

"Thank you, Pete. My wife and I are going to church Sunday. First time in a long time. What happened here, it has made us renew our faith in God. And this time, it's going to last. Pete, do you go to church? If not, you're welcome to go to church with us Sunday."

"I might just do that."

Then Monk leaned to give Pete a hug and looked in his right eye. "Pete, am I nuts? I just saw a young man in dirty street clothes smiling at me from your eye."

"You saw him? Then you know what I was saying was the truth. I will join you Sunday, Monk."

As Pete left, a smile came on his face. "Now I know. Oh yes, I know now. I'm in God's grace."

NEW ORLEANS IS CALLING

A man was traveling from Chicago all the way down to New Orleans. As he sat and looked out the window, he saw the countryside with its small towns and farms going by. He had met, over the years, many interesting people, all from different walks of life. Not once on his trips did he meet anyone rude or hateful. It was a ride he enjoyed—all of them from the time his mom took him from New Orleans to Chicago on his first ride. This would happen twice a year. She worked as a maid, and his father died on a shrimp boat many years back. So his mom, a deeply religious woman, left New Orleans for Chicago for better pay for both. And for her son to get a good education, no scrubbing floors or working on a shrimp boat like his dad.

She saved enough money to go back home and take a few gifts to family. She did this for many years. She said she loved it when on the train she could sit anywhere she liked. Over the years, the countryside changed those small towns. They grew to small cities. Some of the farms, they were sold. Now there were new homes in the fields where corn and cotton grew. Over the years, she changed jobs, with much more pay. She put her son through college, and he earned a degree after a few years. He landed a very good-paying job. He made his mother retire and moved in with him. Taking care of his mom and working six days a week, he had no time for anything else. On Sundays he would drop his mom off at church. Church life was not for him.

Twice a year, he would send his mom back home. His job to hear him say kept him busy. So he had to stay. Then ten years back at Christmas she was going back home. She wanted him to accompany her. He could have, but he just said no. He took her to the station, kissed her.

"Take your time, come back when you feel like it. I'll be here. Next spring, I'll go with you. We will spend a month."

She stayed all the way through New Year; then on her way back around midnight, the angel came and took her away. No one knew she had died until they arrived at the station. They thought she was asleep. It broke his heart, for she was all he had. He ached because he didn't go with her but could have. So within the week, he accompanied his mother back home on the same train that they both had ridden on for many years. On her final trip, he sat in the same seat, the one in which the angel came to take her home. Her funeral was in the tradition of New Orleaner. After a few days, he returned to Chicago. The house was empty, but he kept her room just the way it was the day she left for home. Now after ten years, he's going back to pay her a visit ten years to the day. The same car, same seat. He wondered what she was thinking just before she was taken away. He smiled, and just maybe she would have wanted it that way.

Home, he paid her a visit. With roses, her favorite. Then he visited the family. Yes, he had a good time. It would have been better if she were still around. Then his aunt, her sister, pulled him to one side. She was a minister of the church. Some still believed in the spirits, praying to them alongside praying to God.

"I saw your mom the other night. She was smiling, all dressed in white, standing on a bridge next to a bright light. She was talking. I could not hear what she said. Then I saw you smiling, getting off the train."

He knew people had dreams, but his aunt said, "I saw. I did not dream."

He asked her, "Are they the same?"

"No, son. Dreams are dreams. Most that's what it is. Visions. They are to be reckoned with. I don't know what it means. I believe it has something to do with you."

He stayed over a week and went to see his mom every day. On the last day, he placed one red rose. That rose was from his heart.

"I'll be back next year. I promise," he said as he wiped away the tears. Saying good-bye to the family, he got aboard the train, and as usual, he sat down in the same seat she used on her last trip. Four hours. Outside of Chicago, it was dark. He was alone in the car, thinking that Chicago was his home, but New Orleans was calling. Something inside was calling and saying "come back home" as tears formed in his eyes and ran down his cheek. For some reason, he got up and sat in the other seat. Why he did it, he didn't know. Then a light appeared on the seat where his mom sat. Small at first, then it grew large. Then he remembered what his aunt said.

"Mom, is that you?"

The light said nothing, but something deep inside said she was with him, that she had something to tell him before she would go over to the other side. Then the window came aglow. His mom appeared, all dressed in white. There was a smile on her face.

"Son, I have waited for your return. It's been ten years. He gave a message to your aunt. He wants you to return home, and so do I. For a bad thing will happen. It will affect you all. You will be there to give the people a hand. The one in the light, you know who he is. He will be with you to the end. Then one day, only the Father knows when, on that day, if you believe, you will be with me on the other side."

As she finished, the light got very bright as he saw his mother's spirit being carried into the light. Now it's been four months. He was smiling as he stepped down from the train. His aunt ran and gave him a hug, saying, "Welcome home, son."

Now with his aunt on his side, his business was to help others like he did in Chicago. Then his mind went back to what his mom said. Things will happen, bad things. When that happens, we must be prepared. But this time, no matter what happens to him or New Orleans, he knows he will have God on his side.

THE REUNION

A man in his late thirties was traveling from town to town, seeking work, any kind to put food in his stomach. He was also looking for a place to lay down. The man had been an orphan from the time he was five and shuffled from one foster home to another. He never gave anybody any trouble and kept to himself most of the time. He knew who his mother was. Her name and what she looked like when they took him away. Besides her looks, there was a small tattoo on her left side of her neck in the shape of two hearts with the instructions SS and GS and the word *love* in between. His mom was only twelve when he was born. From all accounts and what he overheard, his grandparents said she was raped by a member of a gang. She didn't know who he was, only what he wore. She was afraid and didn't tell anyone, kept it from all including her parents, until it was time.

Her parents took care of them both after he was born. At fifteen and a teen, it was hard. Other kids made fun of her, calling her teenage mom. Her parents never forgave her for what she did. Then one day, a friend gave her that tattoo with SS and GS with the word *love* in between. That tattoo, it broke the camel's back—they kicked her out along with her son. She was alone on the street. Just her and her son. Soon after, her parents moved. She didn't know where. They went from shelter to shelter; from friend to friend she would stay. Soon she did bad things just to keep her and her son alive. She was afraid to go to the police, heard rumors what they would do. Then word got around. Child services came and took her son. As he was taken away, she cried out.

"As God be my judge, I'm going to find you someday."

From one foster home after another, he was pushed around. As he grew older and could get around on his own, he went back to where they took him, but no one knew who she was, even the tattoo he described. For the area had gone from bad to worst. So after years of foster care, he vowed he would find his mom even if it would take all his life. He finished school with high marks, with no money for college, so he worked at different jobs, took night courses, and finally landed a good job. Then he went to city college, took courses at night, got a degree, and it seemed everything was all right. Then without warning, the banks and everything else just went belly-up including his job. He had a degree, a few dollars in the bank, but with high rent and cost of living, it was eating him away.

So he packed his bags, got on a bus, and said maybe he would try the Southwest, yes, the Southwest. That's where he'll start next. He traveled by bus from town to town. Staying a week or a month, working for board, and keeping the little pay. This would help him until he got back on his feet. New Mexico to him was a million miles away. His mind sometimes would go back. On their bedroom wall, she had a printout of the Grand Canyon. He remembered her saying, "One day I'd like to take you there, away from all this."

His job in the city was an engineer with water and sewer. He was not on top of the seniority, so he was let go. Finally, he arrived at the Grand Canyon area of New Mexico. All he had was a pack, his degree, and other papers where he worked and around five hundred dollars saved up. He needed to get a job. That money would go toward rent, so he decided to sleep under the stars. They were so bright and yet so far away. As he was gazing up, he saw a meteorite streaking across the sky. Then as tears formed in his eyes, he could see his mom crying and waving good-bye as if it were yesterday. He could hear those last words she said, "as God be my judge." Then, for the first time in a long time, as he cried, he started to pray. As he prayed, it seemed like it took all night. Then he fell asleep.

As he slept, he saw his mother waving good-bye like all dreams. But this dream, it stood still. But for his mom, as she smiled, she started to age. He knew his mom was fifty-two, and then she stopped. He could see her as she might look like today. Then the sun came up, and he awoke, but the dream, it didn't go away. That morning he went into the small town. Most of the people were tourists. As he looked around, he thought that just maybe this town was the place to settle down, providing he could get a job. But in the desert, with his degree in water and sewage, it would be unlikely as far as he could see. So he stopped in a diner, had breakfast, and asked where he could apply for work. They told him city hall, just up the street. After filling out papers and talking to a man in charge, everything seemed in order.

"I called back east to check you out. Your boss said you had a good head on those shoulders. We need someone to help bring water in. We use more than what we have. You know, tourists. The lot."

"Give me a few days."

"It's not much pay."

"Do you have a place to stay?"

"No."

"Good. I'll call Hearts Inn. It's a bed-and-breakfast. The owner is very nice. Once you meet her, you won't leave."

"So she's that nice?"

"Oh yes. Came from back east almost thirty years back, married a local. He died, no kids."

"It's strange you talk about kids."

Tears came into her eyes. "Her place is on the right about eight blocks down. If there's no answer, go to the back." He leaves.

"Hope she has a room."

The door was open when he arrived, like any inn. He went inside. In the entry was a sign-in desk and a chair, very neat. On the wall, hanging near the desk, was a printout of the Grand Canyon, just like the one hanging, as he recalled, in their room when he was a kid. No one knew he was around, so he went out in the back. He saw a woman on her knees, planting flowers.

"Excuse me, I understand you may have a room to rent out."

"Yes, I do," she said as she stood and turned around. Then their eyes met. They were frozen in time. This woman was from his dream. Before he could speak, she cried out. "Gene, is that you?"

Then time stood still. When she came forward, he saw the tattoo, those two hearts with SS and GS on her neck. They both then knew their prayers were answered. As they embraced, only tears and laughter could be heard. Then she backed up and looked him over. Her words were, "As God be my judge, I knew you would come to me someday."

It had been weeks now. The town hired him right away. They both shared what happened after that tragic day. She never saw her parents again.

"I tried for years to find you. They told me it was a dead end. Seven years after they took you, I didn't want to go. I moved here, got a job, met my husband. I told him everything. To him it was all right. This house had been in his family for many years. Now it's an inn. He used his clout, went back east, but you just slipped through the cracks. So I found that print, hung it up, hoping you would remember." Then she told him, "The night before you came back into my life, I had a dream. This dream. I saw you as a boy. Then the dream froze, except for you—you started to age, then I woke up. Then you stood behind me. When I saw you, you were the same man as in my dream."

So on the following Sunday, together for the first time in thirty-four years, they held hands and went to church. Everybody heard for the first time. Now the townsfolk know why tears would form in her eyes when they talked about their kids. Now she could smile with tears of joy. She had her son now. Only one could separate them. And she prayed. It would take another lifetime. To God she prayed. No one but him would separate her from her son again.

THE YARD SALE

A man driving down the street stopped at a yard sale. There were lots of items scattered about the yard. A man sitting at a small table said "Hi, look around. If you see anything, let me know."

He had never stopped at any yard or garage sale before. Why now? Why today? As he looked at the owner, the owner gave him that smile that seemed to never go away, and it stayed permanent in your mind. Then he noticed a small oil painting in an old beat-up frame. Dirty, hard to see what it was, so he asked.

"Oh, it's been in the attic for over a hundred years." The house was his grandparents', but now it was his and his wife's home. They were selling a lot of items to pay the bills, unexpected bills. As he talked, that smile was still there. He laid the painting down and looked around again. He picked up five more items, and with the painting, he asked how much. With his smile, he said, "How much will you give for a good cause?"

Without thinking, he pulled out his wallet and gave the man five bills. The man smiled and said, "That seems fair." He wrapped the items and then he left. As he drove off, he looked back and saw the items in the yard. There was no man, just a flash of bright light. At the office, he looked at the items he bought. The only thing that looked good was the painting. It was small, less than nine-by-twelve inches, plus a beat-up wooden frame. As he looked closer, he saw a signature and date. He thought to himself, "I spent five hundred dollars on these items. I can't believe this."

The painting was the only thing that looked halfway good. The rest were knickknacks. Around three the next day, he called one of his friends and told him what he bought and the name and date of the artist. His friend said that the name, he had heard of it before. A few days later, his friend said, "Send a letter and pictures to some of the high-end auction companies or e-mail them. I think you have a winner."

Within a week, an auction house got in touch with him. It was worth quite a bit. At least half a million or better. So he packed it and sent it to the auction. The auction was to be held in six to eight weeks. He thought, as the saying went, "I'm going to make a killing on this sale."

But something was bugging him from somewhere deep down inside. That night, all he could think of was the painting, the smiling man, and what he said. "You're helping a good cause." He couldn't get it out of his mind. Finally, he drove past the house, and there was a foreclosure sign in the yard. At the office, he made a few calls. Yes, the house was in foreclosure. The auction date was in eight weeks. Then after seven weeks, he received word that the painting had fetched four times what the auction house was expecting. He would net way over a million after taxes were taken out.

Now he could quit work and do what he wanted to do, but the images, they kept appearing. Of the smiling man, the house, and what he said. Then the day arrived. The auction of the house, yes, he was there at the courthouse. The auctioneer said the house was totally restored with add-ons. The starting price was 450. No one put their hands up. Within minutes, he said the bank would take offers, no minimum required. When it hit 120,000, he raised his hand. "Sold," the auctioneer said, "Sir, pay up here. The occupants have ten days to leave from today. They will receive the letter to vacate. If not, they will be evicted."

Then he asked himself, "Why? Why did I buy that house? A steal, but I already have one."

Then he asked the bank officer, after giving him the check paid in full, "What about the owners?"

"Oh, you don't know about the Wilsons? That house was built by his grandfather in 1900. Been in the same family. Then young Wilson, his wife, came in and got a loan to restore it the way it was back then. They were good customers, but business is business. He had no life insurance. Driving last winter, he hit a patch of black ice and ran off the road. He was killed at the scene and left his wife and small—yes, four small—kids. Everybody helped. He was the pillar of the neighborhood. Then money ran out. Even her job, something I didn't want to do, but I'm only an officer at the bank, not the CEO. At the price you paid for it, I'm sure Mrs. Wilson could make payments. As you said, you don't need another house."

That night, all he could think of was Mrs. Wilson and the four kids being evicted and with nowhere to go. Then the face of the man, smiling at him, saying, "You know what to do."

The next morning, instead of going to work, he rang on the bell at the Wilsons. A woman answered with swollen eyes. She had been crying, and an eviction notice was on the door.

"Yes?"

"Are you Mrs. Wilson?"

"Yes, I am."

"May I come in?"

"My name is Thomas Ells. I bought this house at auction yesterday."

"I'll be out in ten days, sir, or sooner, but please come in inside."

The house was spotless, with lots of boxes sitting around.

"I'm sorry about the loss of your husband. I didn't know. I spoke with the bank after the sale."

"Sir, we'll be out as soon as we can."

"No. Mrs. Wilson, you're not moving. I already have a home. I'm not married, and I have two houses. No, I'm lucky to take care of one. It's been in your family for over one hundred years. It shall continue. So I'm going to hand the deed of the house free and clear over to you. One more thing. The day you had the yard sale, I bought some items. I paid the man five hundred. He thanked me and said it was for a good cause. He seemed nice. Was he your husband's brother? He kept smiling."

"That day, guess I was in the kitchen cleaning up one of the kids, when I went outside under a small stone on the table was five one-hundred-dollar bills. I thought someone stopped by and left the money. No name."

"I bought six items, all knickknacks, but for one small painting, one of a little girl."

"Yes, that one had been in this house since it was built. Tim, my husband, found it behind a wallboard when we were cleaning the attic to put insulation in. He said one day she would bring us luck. He hung it in the entry."

"Do you have a picture of your husband?"

"Yes, that's him on the mantel."

When Thomas saw the picture, then he knew the smiling man was her husband. Then he told her he was driving down this street. It was his first time, and why he was driving there, he still didn't know.

"That's when I saw a man, your husband, sitting at the table. I slowed down, and he smiled and nodded. I almost hit a car. I parked, looked back, but your husband—I'm sorry, that man that looked like your husband—had an aura all around him, a very bright glow. When I approached him, the aura went away. After I bought the items, he said it was for a good cause. As I was ready to pull away, I looked back. All I saw was a flash of bright light. No one was around. Then I saw him in my dreams. That's when I drove by and saw the auction sign. So now I know what I must do."

Within minutes, they both seemed like old friends. That's when he told her what the painting brought. He gave her half less the cost of the house. Mrs. Wilson said, "Now Tim, I pray, will rest in peace." From that moment on, Thomas saw Tim no more.

Miracles do happen, and they come in many forms. It's been four years now. Thomas had sold his house and moved in with the Wilsons. Oh, did I forget to say that two years after he rang the doorbell they were married and now have another kid? They named him Tim, and as Thomas would say, if Tim was watching, he would approve and be smiling from the other side.

FATHER MEETS SON

A young man of twenty applied for work at a construction site. He was hired on the spot. To the office and other workers, it seemed strange. Usually their boss took his time when hiring and would check everyone out. He always dotted his i's and crossed his t's. This time, after looking at the applicant's résumé, the boss hired him on the spot. "My name is Bill Mathews. I'm the owner. The foreman is not here today. Fill out the employment forms and give it to Sue. I'll see you tomorrow at seven sharp. If you're late, don't come at all." Then Mr. Mathews left.

After filling out the forms, he handed them to Sue. "Sue, my name is Bob, Bob Bakker."

"I'm Sue Smidth. You're one lucky guy. Mr. Mathews always checks out the people he hires. It takes up to four days. But with the look on his face, it was surely different this time. So welcome to Mathews construction."

Bob left and returned to his one-room apartment or flophouse. It was not in the best part of town. He had a coffeepot and hot plate. He opened a can of soup and drank his coffee and lay down to get some sleep. It had been hard for him. He was out of work for some time, pounding the pavement day after day. It was getting him down. It wasn't his fault that jobs were just hard to find.

As he tried to go to sleep, his mind wandered back as far as he could remember. His mother was small, blonde, with that baby-doll image. She was beautiful and worked very hard six days a week. When he got old enough, she took him to one side and told him her life story. She was an only child. Her parents were old when she was born. Her father was sixty, her mom fifty-two. They tried all their lives to have a child. When finally she was born, to them both it was a godsend, like Sarah and Abraham in the Bible. So they named her Sarah and put a protective shield around her. At their age, they were afraid that they might lose her. She was small even at birth. Over the years, she was still small and was in and out of hospitals. It wore her parents down. When she was seventeen, both of her parents died within three months of each other. She stayed with her aunt for a while and finished school. She wanted to go to college, but her health would say no. So she got a job as a hostess at a very nice restaurant. The owners, they knew her parents very well. That helped a lot.

The year was 1969. The war in Vietnam was in high gear. The draft, there was a lot of protesting. She would hear people say that all hell had broken loose. There were young men being drafted, going to Canada, burning the flag, their draft cards. She lived in Oakland where a lot of soldiers were departing to Nam. She would talk to them. Some nights she would go to the USO dance club with them before they departed. One night after work on a Friday, around eight, she went to the club. Most were just guys she danced with. There were no names, just faces. Then one young man asked her to dance. He was awkward and kept stepping on her shoes. He said he never danced before.

"OK," she said, "tonight is a long night. Before it's over, you will know how to dance and sweep the girls off their feet." She showed him, and at 3:00 a.m., they left together. It was her first, for she always went home alone. But this man was totally different. He did as she said, and he swept her off her feet. Walking down the street, they stopped in an all-night carryout and deli and had a bite to eat. An arcade machine was there, so they took some pictures of them smiling and holding each other. He was a hunk of a man with that uniform on. Afterward, without thinking, she invited him up to her place. Inside, they kissed. She told him she never did this before. He smiled and told her the same. "I'm a farm boy from back east," he said.

The next day, they cut the shots in two, and each had three. She gave him her address and said, "When you get back, look me up."

Then he left. He was leaving that night. That was the last time she saw or heard from him. Then a son was born. She named him Bob Bakker, after her father. Somewhere along the way, names were forgotten. She raised her son, never got married, and the memory of that soldier, his father, stayed with her. Yes, it was hard to believe, but to her it was love at first sight. He remembered seeing the photos of her and her father. Then when he was fifteen, she got very sick, and she asked him to put the photos with her. He knew what she meant.

The next day, holding her hand, the angel came and took her away. He put the photos with her. All but one, which he kept. Afterward, he went to live with his other great-aunt, finished school, and wanted to go to college. But he had no funds, so he had to work. So he struck out on his own. It was 1989. Up and down the coast, he went applying for work of any kind. He had no experience, just a strong body and a keen mind and the determination to make it like his mom, with God's help, one day at a time.

Before he fell asleep, he asked God to keep him safe and be with him to help and show him the way to live right one day at a time. Bright and early the next morning, Bob was at work before the others arrived. The foreman introduced himself and showed him what to do, carry this, cut that. He was a jobber; anything that required no experience, he did. This went on for four months. He worked hard and showed up on time, cleaned up the mess. Everyone was impressed. Some offered to take him out for a beer. His reply was that he didn't drink, smoke, or do any drugs. Some asked why. He replied that he was brought up that way. He remembered his mother saying that his father said the same thing, saying it would ruin your life. Then the foreman told him he was getting a raise, for him to move out of that one-room apartment. With his raise, he could afford a better place closer to work.

Within a year, he was learning a trade he liked. But over his shoulder, he could sense Mr. Mathews was watching him. This went on for almost two years. He advanced. The foreman said he was doing a better job than some who had been in this business for years. Then one day, it was pouring rain. Everyone was sent home. Mr. Mathews asked Bob to stay and have lunch with him. He wanted to get to know him better. He knew Mr. Mathews was never married, yet he knew he was not gay. But something drew them both together. After lunch, he told Bob his story, where he came from. He was a farm boy back east at the time of Vietnam in '69. He was but eighteen and got drafted and went to Nam. He was assigned to the core of engineers. When he got out, he was going back home, back east, when something made him stay.

He had been here ever since. He went to a trade school, then college, and would go home as often as he could. His parents were getting older, so he talked them into selling the farm because developers wanted it for houses. So they sold, moved here, and all three lived together. They bought the house that he was living in today. He took the balance and started this company. His father was a farmer and knew nothing about building homes. So his parents stayed home, enjoying the warm sun. There was no snow to plow, no cows to feed. It was a vacation, twelve months a year.

His parents were older. He was their only child. Then a few years back, his father died. Then a year later, his mom. Bob asked Bill if he was ever married. Then Bill gave him a funny look and said no. Bill said, "It's a long story. It goes way back."

"Since we're talking, would you tell me about it?"

"I don't talk about it often. When I do, I don't finish. I was being shipped out to Nam. On my last night of leave or pass, I went to an USO club in Oakland. I asked a very beautiful young girl to dance. I was stepping all over her shoes. Then we left together. At her place, it was the first time for both of us. The next day, I left. I didn't get back till the end of the war. When I did, I lost her address, lost everything. I met her once and fell in love. That love had lasted to even now. I searched for her for a few years. I figured she got married and moved away. All I have left of her besides the memory of that night are three arcade pictures."

Then Bill looked at Bob. Bob was crying. At the same time, Bob reached into his billfold and pulled out an arcade picture and handed it to Bill. "Is this you?"

Bill could not speak. He got up, took a small old picture out of his billfold and laid it next to the other. They matched. Neither one could speak. All they could do was stare at the pictures and each other. Bob then said, "You're my dad. Mom never married. She was buried with the other two, on her request."

All they could do was hug each other and cry. Then Bill took Bob home with him. All that night, all the way up to the break of dawn, they talked and told each other everything. Bill then told Bob, "On the day you applied for work and I looked into your eyes, I saw your mother's face. I had to leave, so I said you were hired."

"Is that why you were watching me?"

"Yes. You act just like me when I was your age. Look at those pictures. And in the mirror. That could be you. We could have been twins."

Then everyone at work heard the news. Then Bill, with Bob's permission, had his mom moved to his family plot. Bill told Bob, "I will never get married. She was my true love. If God is willing, we'll be together one day on the other side."

Now, many years later, Bob, with his wife and kids, were saying good-bye to his father as they laid him to rest next to his true love, Sarah. He smiled as he walked away. Now, for the first time in forty years, they will meet again and be together with God in paradise on the other side.

GEORGE'S STORY

An old, old man bent with age was watching TV as others around him were saying, "History is being made today. We just elected our first Afro-American president. This is what America is all about."

Without a word, he got up and went out and sat on the porch. As tears formed in his eyes, he smiled, thinking to himself, "Yes, we have elected our first black president. Our first, and he is also half white."

He was ninety-five years old and lived in a home. Still, he had his mind. Even with his stooped shoulders, he was pretty strong. Then he got up and went out into the yard under a large oak tree and sat down on a bench and closed his eyes. He let his mind wander back, back to when he was a very young man. He was a grandson of a slave, now a son of a storekeeper. He remembered it as if it were yesterday, what his grandfather told him. His grandfather was about twenty when the War between the States ended. He was lucky he worked in the house. Little by little, with the help of his master's daughter, without the master knowing, she taught him to read and write.

After the war, and because he could read and write, he met a man from the North, from Columbus, Ohio, a carpetbagger selling goods from the North or trading goods to take back. The man from Ohio was named Hale. He told Jim, "If you can read and write, I'll pay you. I need someone, a go-between. Us from the North, you folks from the South."

So the two struck a bond, a bond that grew into a lifelong friendship. Jim told Mr. Hale that his father was the foreman of the plantation. He had raped his mother when she was fifteen. Nothing was ever done unless the owner of the slaves pressed charges. It happened all the time back then. So that was how it started between Jim and Mr. Hale. Within two years, they were sending items back and forth by train. Then one day, Mr. Hale told Jim he was opening a store in Ohio. Their business was expanding, getting large. Without a word, Mr. Hale gave Jim a legal paper, making him a full partner. In case of either's death, the other would receive the company and its assets lock, stock, and barrel. Mr. Hale never got married, never talked to Jim about his family, never cussed, never drank. On Sundays he would go to church, any church, no matter where they were staying. The closest one, white or black church, it didn't matter.

Then Jim, on one of his trips to the South, met a young woman ten years younger. They got married. He moved her to Ohio to be close to the store, and she worked at the store and had four kids. The first was a boy, and they named him George, after Mr. Hale, that was his father. George Washington Lincoln Meads. Their partnership lasted for over thirty years. George was much older than Jim by at least thirty years. Then George got sick, which the doctor said was just a cold. He lay in bed for over two weeks and could hardly talk or move. Bess, Jim's wife, took care of George and nursed him back to health, but George never fully recovered. So most of the company's affairs were left to Jim.

One afternoon, George called Jim to his side. He told Jim, "We've been together for over thirty years. We never got mad at each other, never said a harsh word. You know my name. That's all you ever ask. Now I will tell you the story, the whole story, the story of my life. The one you never ask about. My name is Hale, George Hale. I'm from Columbus by way of New Orleans. My mother, her maiden name was Hale, not by marriage. Her name was Rebecca Hale. She was born and raised in New Orleans. Her parents were not rich, had no slaves. They were clothiers. They had a shop and sold clothes from England and France. Also, they were good at making evening gowns and tuxedos for their rich clients. Rebecca, my mom, was not like the others she knew. She treated everyone the same, rich or poor. Even the slaves.

"Then she met a black slave, a servant of a rich family who dealt in cotton. They sold most of the cotton to England and France. Then one thing led to another, and she became pregnant. She cancelled it right up to the time of delivery. No one knew. Her parents were furious. After the birth, she asked what the baby looked like. They told her the baby was male, had blond hair and blue eyes. Jim, that baby was me. I'm half black, same as you. My mother never told me my father was a slave. Even my father never knew. She told her parents she went to one of those dances, met a man from out of town, just gave a name, that's all she knew. He asked her out, and there he took advantage of her. She never told no one. She said she never saw him again. Her parents accepted it, but to others, that was her downfall. So my mother never dated, never married, and raised me, her son, as white.

"I went to school, made good grades, helped in the store. Then when I was around twenty, I talked my grandfather into letting me go North to get a route started so we could buy, sell, or trade and we could make more money, have enough money for your old age, I never cared about sewing, nor did my mom. Just buy and sell. Then there was the friction between the North and South. I was home when my grandfather died. Then within six months, Grandma died from a stroke, so the business was left to my mom. We ran it for almost a year. Then Mom pulled me to one side and told me the whole story.

At first I was mad, real mad. Then she asked me not to tell no one, for if anyone found out, no one would do business with us again. Around a month later, a man from Paris came in and offered to buy the business. After a few negotiations, we decided to sell and move to Columbus where I had established a small business. And the amount we settled on was enough to start all over again. We had a small house with a shop and had enough to hire a seamstress.

"I traveled, and Mom took care of the store. Then it was hard to get items from the South. Every trip I took, I brought back less. Then the war started. What little work we had went to the army. Pay was few and far between. Then Mom got sick with a bad fever, and she never pulled through. Before she died, a smile came on her face. She told me one day I would meet a man, a black man who could read and write. She said, 'He will be your companion through your entire life. You will know him, for he will be half white.' Then she smiled, squeezed my hand, and her face lit up like the glowing of the sun. Then she asked me, 'Do you see the light? It's calling my name.' Then she died. And that light, it went inside me and changed me forever, for I had kept this bitterness bottled up inside all those years. Then I sold the business. It was near the end of the war. Then one evening, I took a very hot bath. The room was steamy. As I was ready to shave, the mirror was all steamed up. I started to wipe it clean. That's when I saw a face, your face. Then I knew. So when we met, I knew what my mom said, and it was true."

The next day, Jim talked to Bess and told her everything. Then they told the kids. That's when they all decided to change their name from Mead to Hale. And as a gift to George, they showed him the papers. They took his name, and Jim became George's son. Then later, George died. Jim and his family lost a friend and, yes, Jim lost his dad.

So now George Jr. looks out across the yard. He remembers it so well, his grandfather's story. And as he told it, tears would roll down his cheeks. Before his grandfather died, he told young George that one day, maybe in your lifetime, not mine, a black man would become president. And then he smiled and said, "And I bet, by all accounts, he will be half white."

OLD BOB

There was a man, I've been told, who lived back during the Depression. No one knew anything about him, and he just went by Old Bob. Bob was old, even then, as the story went. Old Bob would travel up and down the countryside, seeking work, a place to sleep, and maybe a few good meals. Old Bob had two companions who never left his side. One was a large dog that, they said, a ten-year-old could ride. The other was a cat, which was very small in weight, no more than ten pounds.

When you asked Bob about the odd pair, he would tell you a few years back when he had a job and a home, he found Jack when he was a small pup. Someone or something had beaten the pup so bad that he could hardly move, but after much loving care, Jack grew to what he was now. They formed a bond. To get to Bob, you had to go through Jack. Then his wife of fifty years died. The Depression came, and he lost everything. All he had to his name was Jack, so they, like a lot of other people, went from place to place, seeking work of any kind.

Then about two years back, as the two were walking by the railroad tracks, Jack heard something and went running. When he came back, he had this small black-and-white kitten in his mouth. He laid it down at Bob's feet. The kitten was cute and was the size of a fist. It must have strayed from its mom. So Bob started to leave, but Jack, in his own way, stayed with the kitten. So Bob put the kitten in his pocket after feeding her what little food they had. The three formed a partnership, as strange as it might have seemed. He named the cat Jill. Jack was large, a total mixed breed, and Jill was small enough that she could lay on Jack's back and go to sleep.

Bob would travel the hill country where the people there were friendlier than the townsfolk. He would do work around the house or barn. He plowed the fields. No matter where he was at or what he did, Jack and Jill would be by his side. Then on one of his stops, he met a widower with a small farm. Her family lived on other farms close by. She offered him a job. Her husband, like Bob's wife, had died a few years back. She buried him on the farm in a family cemetery. The farm had been in the family for over a hundred years. When you looked out from the back porch, you could see it up on the hill. Bob said yes and fixed up a place in the barn. Her name was Hanna Brown. Mrs. Brown and her children liked old Bob. The little ones would ride Jack. They all got alone just fine.

Hanna asked Bob about his life. All he would give was his name, Bob Crawford. To Hanna, Bob's past was his own. But Bob would tell her some stories about the three. A year ago, it was starting to get cold. They had nothing to eat. They were well off the beaten path when he noticed that Jill was missing. He looked high and low, and even Jack joined in. But they guessed that her scent was gone. She was gone all night. Neither he nor Jack slept that night. They just huddled with each other as it started to snow. Then as the snow started to stick on the ground, Jack jumped up and started running. Within minutes, Bob saw Jill with Jack, who had a large rabbit in her mouth. He fixed the rabbit and fried it with lard he had in his pack. Strange as it seemed, Jack nor Jill wouldn't eat raw meat; it had to be cooked. Maybe it was Bob's doing. He would share his meal with both. He would smile and say that they were more human than some humans he had met.

Then he told her one that afternoon, two men attacked Bob. They thought he might have a buck or two. They didn't see Jack or Jill. When it was over, one man had claw marks all over his back, and the other had teeth marks in his cheeks. He laughed and said that they ran faster than a deer. That's the way it was with Bob, Jack, and Jill. He told Hanna he was near eighty. And when the man came calling, what would happen to his companions? She told him everything would be all right.

Then one morning, Jack ran to the house, barking very loud. Hanna went as fast as she could to the barn. Jill was sitting on Bob's lap. He was in a chair. The man he spoke of finally came. The family buried Bob in the cemetery on the hill. Jack and Jill knew what happened in their own special way, so Hanna took them in. But every morning, noon and night, both of them would lay on old Bob's grave. This went on for ten years after Bob had died. Then Jack, in his old age, died one morning, lying on old Bob's grave. The only thing Hanna could do was ask the family to put Jack in a wooden box, dig a hole, and bury Jack in the same grave as Bob's.

Jill kept up the mourning and would sleep with Hanna, but every day Jill would go to the grave and lay down for a spell. Cats live longer, so they say. Hanna had Jill for another ten years. Then they buried Jill in the same manner as Jack. Now it has been at least eighty years. Hanna was buried next to her husband. Her children still has the farm. And the cemetery, it's mowed and flowers planted. It was a perfect resting place. The stone on old Bob's grave reads "Bob Crawford, Died March 15, 1935. Companions: Jack, Died April 20, 1945, Jill, Died March 1, 1955.

Now it has been many, many years later as the story goes. On certain days and time, if you look up on the hill, you can see old Bob sitting on his grave with his two companions, Jack and Jill, by his side.

THE HIGHWAY

A man was driving down a lone stretch of highway and had a long way yet to go. It was late at night in the pouring rain. Nothing was in sight, not even a house. When he was going over a hill, he saw someone walking, all soaking wet. He passed the man and then slowed down. To himself, he said, "I must give this man a ride."

He opened the door and asked the man to get in and out of the rain. The man got in, all soaking wet and looking pale. The driver said, "My name is Ben. I haven't been down this road in many a year. Not since I was a teen."

The other said, "I am Joe. Joe Black is my name."

A few miles down the road, Joe said, "If you don't mind, I have a story to tell. Over fifty years ago this day, to be precise, a man was walking down this road. It was raining just like now. He had lost his job, his car, and he was hitchhiking, trying to get back home to his mom and dad to be with them on the farm. He had left the farm a few years back and wanted to make it big in the city to send some money back. He did all right for a while, then no more work to be had. Everybody got laid off. He lost his job, his car, so he decided to go back to where he belonged, back home to Mom and Dad on the farm. He had a long way to go. Most used the new freeway, but it was out of the man's way. As he was walking that night, everything went black. He was hit by a car that was coming over the hill and going very, very fast. The man was killed there on the spot, but the driver kept on going, didn't slow down, didn't look back. He was still traveling very fast.

"Somewhere along the way, the man lost his wallet, so he had no id. So they buried him in a potter's field, John Doe number four. That's also the name they gave him on the stone. That happened fifty years ago this night. The man, he still walks this stretch of highway, hoping to meet the man that hit him. And he would not stop but continue on his way."

As Joe looked at Ben, he said, "You are that man. I have longed and waited to see you and ask why you didn't stop and help."

Now Ben, old in his age, came to a sudden stop, trying to speak. No words would come out. But his mind went back to that night. He was only a teen, not old enough to drink, but he did. Got drunk, all because of a spat he had with his girl. He came down this road, now he recalled, coming over the hill. He thought he saw and hit a deer. He kept on going; it was only a deer, after all. Now he could see it all. The man next to him was the man he killed fifty years past. He started to cry.

"I didn't know it was you, I thought it was a deer. I was drunk, out of my mind. Oh my God, what am I to do?"

Joe, all wet and pale, smiled at him and said, "I've waited fifty years to meet you and tell you what you did. I forgive you, but there is one thing you must do, for I don't want to walk this highway anymore. Go to where they buried me and put my name, Joe Black on the stone. My mom and dad are gone now. They are waiting for me someway beyond."

Ben said, "I will do as you ask. I'm sorry for what happened that night, fifty years past."

Then the rain stopped, and a bright light was in front of the car. Joe smiled, and he became all dressed in white. He said, "Now I'm ready to go to the other side. Then he went into the light."

Ben, now seventy-eight years old, sat behind the wheel and said, "Am I dreaming this? Is this for real?"

Then something from deep down inside told him that what he had seen was for real. As he looked to where Joe was sitting, a wallet lay open with Joe's ID and a picture of Joe's mom and dad. He picked the wallet up and did what Joe asked him to do. And Ben did one more thing. Whether they believed him or not, he had the wallet as proof. He will tell the police; then they should do what they must. And he will do one more thing. He will rebury Joe next to his mom and dad.

THE MAN THAT DID NOT BELIEVE

A man was lying in bed and thinking about what would happen to his family after he was dead. Yes, he was like a lot of people. He believed that once you were dead, you were dead.

He had his will made out for quite some time. All the i's dotted and the t's crossed. His wife, his kids, they—once he is gone—will all be financially well-off.

He then closed his eyes and fell asleep. When he opened them, he was wide awake. His room, it looked different, but yet the same. He got out of bed, went downstairs, and he heard voices coming from the living room just down the hall. He looked in and saw his family with all his friends. Most of them were dressed in black. He asked himself, "What's going on? And why is everybody dressed this way, in black?"

Then he heard one say to his wife, "We're sorry for your loss."

Then he realized he must be dead. He went and knelt in front of her. "Hun, look at me. Can't you see I'm alive? I'm alive. I can't be dead."

Then a voice came to him, saying his name. "Yes, you are dead, and this is no game. Now you are dead and still walking around. Remember what you believed, that once you're dead, you're dead. For this is what happens to people who don't believe. Some walk throughout their home both day and night, never at rest. Seeing their family but they can't see them. Until one day, they move out and others move in. You lose your contact. You want to go with them, but you can't. So you will walk these floors day in and day out even when this house is turned down and maybe a high-rise put in its place. This will go on and on until, yes, judgment day. But oh, I'm sorry, you don't believe. You and others like you are the lucky ones. You had a great life, loved your family. Gave a lot to the needy. But still, you don't believe. Others are not so lucky. Come, I'll show you and what they are going through."

And he saw. He saw them all. They were crying out in such pain no man alive could endure.

The voice said, "They have done things far worse than you. What you just saw, it was not the worst by far. Would you like to see it all?"

"No, no, please, no. I can't bear even to see this."

Then the voice said, "What would you want me to do? Send you back before you were dead?"

The man started to cry from deep, deep down inside.

"I didn't believe because there was no proof."

"The only proof you needed was faith, and it comes from inside."

Then a light brighter than the sun and the voice that also came from within the light said, "I am *he* that was dead. I am the one that you denied. Now you want me to send you back. Look at all these souls here. I'm not sending them back. Why should I send you?"

The man answered and said, "Lord, you are right. I was wrong. Please forgive me and do with me as you wish. I deserve this, like the others, for I did not believe."

The voice then said, "I cannot send you back because you are not dead. Though you are dead in your heart, I came into your dream like all these others. When they awoke, they still didn't believe. And when that time finally came, now you see where they are at. They will be here till judgment and beyond. Now it's up to you. Do what's right."

The man opened his eyes, his body all soaking in sweat, and got up and went downstairs. His wife of fifty years smiled at him, saying, "Is everything all right?"

He smiled back, saying, "Remember what you always wanted me to do? Tomorrow is Sunday. Let's go to church and worship God and his Son together for the first time."

For miracles do happen, for one just happened.

Will a miracle similar to this happen to you?

THE STUDENT

A man left his family and struck out on his own. His family was strict: smoking, drinking, or cussing was prohibited. He obeyed his parents. His friends, on the other hand, would not come around. They called his parents old-fashioned.

He lived in a small town, with farms all around. His parents owned a hardware store. He worked there on weekends. During the summer, he worked at a couple of farms and saved his money for college. Then that day came. It was time for him to leave. Holding back the tears, he said good-bye to them both and got on a bus headed for the city and to school. He would see the other side of life. He enrolled at a small city college, studying management. After two years, he transferred to state. At state, he soon found out he had a long way to go. There were different people, a different atmosphere. Then, like a lot of young people, he started hanging out with the wrong crowd. At first it was a beer, then two. Soon he was drinking every night. That led to him doing a little weed, and that led to smoking it every night.

Before he knew it, he was losing interest in his studies and even in school. He started working longer hours just to pay for his habit. Finally, he dropped out of school altogether. His parents would call, but one excuse led to another. Then one night, he got so high. He was rushed to the ER. They worked on him for over an hour, pumped his stomach, trying to get the drugs out of his system. Then it happened like a lot of times in the ER. But instead of him dying, he went into a coma. They put him in ICU, hoping their drugs would counter the ones he took. All they could do was wait, hope, and yes, pray that something better would happen. In a lot of cases it did; then in some cases, it didn't. God works a lot of times. He uses us to help others. In the end, we call it a miracle.

Tom, the young man, was good at heart. Even though he got on drugs, he never used God's name in vain and still went to church on Sundays.

The crowd he hung around with never came by at the ER or even to see him in ICU. As Tom lay in a coma, the hospital was trying to get in touch with his parents. Something happened. Deep down inside of Tom, that part we call the soul or spirit, something moved. It made Tom sit up, but only inside. His body still lay motionless. Then he saw his greatest fear. He was in a pit, a bottomless pit so deep that it started pulling him down. All he could hear were voices screaming in his ear, crying out, "No, no. No more. I can't take the pain."

But it got worse. The farther he descended, the worse it got. Then he opened his eyes. What he saw was his worst fear coming before him, and he started to scream. But he prayed to God instead. Then he saw his body floating, and finally he was at his parents' home. He was at the foot of their bed. They awoke, startled. He held his hands out to them, saying, "Help me please." Then his spirit prayed to God in the Son's name, and he was back in his body. He opened his eyes. When the vision came clear, his parents were by his side. The doctors and nurses were smiling with pride.

His parents embraced him like they never did before. Then when all was quiet, he asked them, "So the doctors got through to you?"

With tears in their eyes, they said, "No, you did."

Then they told him what happened. A storm had come through. Everything went out, even the phone, so they went to bed early. They didn't know the time, but a bright light appeared to them.

"Then out of the light, we saw you standing at the foot of the bed, asking for help and crying to God. Then you faded. We knew something was wrong. So we drove and came directly to the hospital, not at your apartment. We both felt someone holding our hand, saying, 'Everything will be all right if only you believe.' We have been here for two days. Your eyes kept moving back and forth very fast, but your eyelids were closed shut. Then you finally spoke those words, *Jesus help me*, and you opened your eyes."

Within a week, Tom was discharged and told his parents everything. He left nothing out. Miracles do happen. He had no relapse. Afterward, he went back to school. This time he got in with the right crowd, graduated with a 3.5, and now he works at a large agricultural company that specializes in making crops bigger and more resistant and can grow in severe weather. Yes, he goes home every few month. For three weeks a year he takes off from work without pay and takes over the hardware store while his parents take a break. Yes, miracles do happen. All you have to do is believe.

THE DINER

His name was Gene, and he was sitting in a diner eating his meal. When he looked out the window, he saw a family: a man, a woman, and two kids. They were staring at the people eating their dinner, for in large cities, you see this both day and night. But this was a whole family, so he stopped eating. He could not swallow, for he was all choked up. So without hesitation, he got up, went out, and invited them in. They hesitated, but he insisted. When they sat down, he asked them to order what they wanted. The kids smiled, and the parents nodded. When the meal arrived, without looking, they all bowed their heads and prayed. They thanked the Lord for this meal and asked the Lord to bless the man for what he just did while other patrons looked and turned their heads the other way.

For the first time in a long time, after they said their prayer, he joined in with them to say amen. As he watched them eat, he ordered all a great dessert and told the waitress to fix something so they could take it with them. They talked and told him their story. Both worked—her days, him nights. Then both their jobs took a flight, and they got kicked out for not paying their rent. Out on the streets, it has now been twelve weeks. They slept where they could. They told him they were not the only ones—there were thousands more that blended in, but he didn't see. The kids, eight and nine, didn't understand why their parents lost their jobs. Was it something they did wrong? Then the cook overheard and came over with a smile on his face and asked the mother, "If you can wait tables, you got yourself a job."

She smiled and said, "I'll take it."

And he took her to one side. The father had tears in his eyes and did not know what to say. Then he looked at the father's neck where a cross dangled from a chain, not gold but brass and small, but it shined bright as it hit the man's eyes, and then he knew what he was supposed to do. His place was not far away and with a spare bedroom he had never used. He took them and gave them a home, a place to stay till they got back on their own. And where he worked, an opening was to be filled, a mail-room clerk, not paying a lot but enough. They stayed with him until they got their own place.

Now both of them were working, and the kids were in school. Now as he ate at the diner, Gloria—that's her name—now waits on him with that smile on her face as he walks in and says hello. It made it all worthwhile just to see her and her family smile. Besides, with what he did, they changed his life in ways he didn't understand. He prayed to God now. He had never done this before, just himself and nothing more. For now he had helped others find a place and a job. And he was wondering just what was in it for him. Then his mind wandered back to that day when that cross blinked brightly in his eyes. And then he knew. Before he was just a fool. It was love, true love for his fellow man.

And from a distance, but still close at hand, another looked at him and smiled and said to himself, "A job well done." So this other, he travels from place to place doing to others as he did to Gene.

"For in that time, when all shall be judged, I shall judge you and others like you with truth and a smile on my face."

THE THREE R'S

As I sat and looked at an old 1959 yearbook, I wondered what it would be like to go back to the time of our forefathers when they had to work with their hands and with hardly any machines. Their kids, they had to walk or ride a horse or, if lucky, a buggy to a one-room school. Yet in some parts of our country, that hasn't been that far back. Just imagine, if you can, a one-room school—one teacher, the three r's, that was the rule. Yes, it was a hard time back then compared to now. Our kids today, they have their own cars. And if it weren't for sports, many would stay away. To them, sports, that's all there is.

To their parents, it's the same. Raise the taxes so my kids can play sports. What? What do you mean? To many parents, that's all it means. But to most, it's the three r's, and those three r's will get them far. Imagine if you will, Abraham Lincoln born in a log cabin, self-taught himself mostly those three r's. No sports, and became president of this great nation, this great country of ours. When I went to school, we walked up three flights of stairs. The restrooms or toilets, they were outside, and in the winter, you didn't stay long. There was no heat, so as fast as you could, you ran back inside. We had sports, but that came last.

One other thing that is missing today, kids and teachers, they don't say a prayer or grace or even say "in God we trust." We did. We did it a lot, and I believe it made us, at least most of us, stop and think. Without God, how did our Founding Fathers plainly write it on a piece of paper that's called our constitution and in it it was written one nation under God? God put in the minds and the hearts of our Founding Fathers those words, "in God we trust." It applies to Jews and Gentiles; that includes us all. So now, a few, so very few, those slabs with those words written on them were handed to Moses. From him on down to you and me, they wanted them removed from every public place. Their reason, they don't believe at all in God. As I look back at my old school where I studied grade one through twelve, it was torn down, and a new grade school was put up in its place. Our high school, North Gallia High, it's closed. So now our schools, they have combined from a few into one.

Yes, time changes from year to year, but what should remain is the golden rule, those three *r*'s; they will get you far. Sports is nice to have, but only a few, a very few, will achieve their goal by strictly relying only on sports. So time has changed. Typewriters. What's that? Rotary phone. You used them? Man, how old are you? Some things they have in school now that we didn't have back then? Calculators, BlackBerries, Cell phones. To add or subtract, we used our heads. BlackBerries, that's what I picked in summer.

Ah yes, a lot of things have changed. In years to come, if we're still here, the teens today will have grandkids of their own. And those grandkids will look at them and say, "Grandpa, what's a blackberry? typewriters? rotary phones? I saw them today in a museum. Grandpa, how old did you say you are?" Yes, times have changed. Remember *Sputnik*? When we were in school, then it was the race to the moon. What will it be like a few years down the road? Another gizmo will replace the blackberry, but the schools, the three *r*'s they will be different, taught a different way. But they will still mean the same, so tell your kids, your grandkids, go and finish school. Then on to college or a trade school, get as much education as they can.

For some, and we pray a lot, will one day be like that president born in a cabin, self-taught. Just maybe one from this town or this area, a very small dot on the map, a little place in Ohio County called Gallia. Someone from the place Vinton will become president of this great country of ours. For me, I'm not ashamed like some that have left and gone away and never returned. We were poor farmers. My father was crippled from the mines and worked the farm with two horses. He raised twelve kids. My mom, she loved that farm. That was her home or Morgan Lane. Her past life, she left it behind. Now Vinton she called home, and both of my parents are buried here, and one day so will I. So put God first. In him all things are possible, from those tablets he gave to Moses to his son, and the Sermon on the Mount to our constitution that says one nation under God. Put those back in school, and with those three r's, we can achieve a lot.

HISTORY CHANNEL

A man was seated at his desk, working. He stopped, put his work aside, got up, and stood staring out the window. He wondered to himself, "Is it true? Did we all come from that little speck in the sea? Or were we created by God? This God that is mentioned in the Bible, if you have read it and believe."

He has never read the Bible. Even as a kid going to church, to him the church or other places of worship were a business just like his. The only difference was they were tax exempt. He smiled. They have a good thing going.

He returned to his desk and finished his work. He left to go home to his family and have a quiet dinner, relax, and watch the news and his favorite programs, then off to bed to sleep. After dinner, he watched the news. Halfway through, it got disturbing—the wars, the drugs, the economy. The same old, same old. So what should he do? So he turned on the History Channel. Something old yet new. The history of the Bible from Genesis all the way through.

"Oh, why not?" he thought. "There's nothing else to do." And this just may give him new insight, new discoveries. Yes, he'll watch it. Just maybe he would learn something new. It told of Eden, between four rivers. "So far," he thought, "they have found only two." Then his eyes opened when they said a satellite image of the area showed two other rivers that. at the same point in time, have been dried and covered up. Also, the ocean was five hundred feet below what it was now. "Fascinating," he thought, "I'll watch this all the way through."

Finally, the hour was over. He liked what he had seen and heard. Then a voice came on. "Stay tuned next week, chapter two." This was OK, so he marked it down in his book: "next week history channel chapter two."

So he retired to bed. His wife was already asleep. As he slept, he dreamed about Eden and all the things that Adam and Eve went through. He dreamed of Cain and Abel to Babel and Noah and the ark. When he woke up, he knew what he had dreamed. Before he woke up, something told him that what he dreamed was true. But what? He shrugged it off. He's had dreams of things he had seen on TV before, but this one, this dream, it was so real.

Two days later, there was a rerun of the same program, so he watched it again. This time, he saw it in a different light. He understood it better, much better than before. He pondered on it all week long until, finally, chapter two. His wife teased him, saying, "You're going to become a fanatic if you keep this up."

As he watched the Bible unfold, week after week, chapter after chapter, he tired. When he slept, he dreamed about what he had seen. So instead of waiting week after week, he ordered the complete set of tapes. That way he could watch as many chapters as he liked. He watched them all from Adam and Eve to Abraham and Moses, through and past David, until he got to a man—the Bible said he is the Son of God. He knew the Christmas story most of us do. It's after that. So what he did, he watched that story all the way through, from the time at the temple to the River Jordan, the temptation and his final deed, dying on the cross, rising from the dead. He watched it all. As tears flowed down his cheeks, he wondered, "Is this man for real? Or just a sad story?"

He watched the rest all the way through, to the last book, the one written by John. As he read John's book, news of the world today flashed before his eyes. Then something from deep, deep down inside made him start to cry. Then something stood in front of him, a light so very bright, and it spoke to him in a soft, gentle voice, "I am the one that was dead but is alive. What you have seen is the truth, not a lie. I am here for you now and will be with you till your end. Then you will be with me. Yes, with me, in paradise forevermore. For I am the way, the truth, and the light. No man cometh to the Father but by me. If only you will believe and accept me without hesitation."

He fell to his knees, asking for forgiveness. As he prayed, a heavy burden was lifted and went away. He felt like a new man. Then the voice said, "I am pleased. I'll be with you always to the end of the world and beyond because now you believe."

As he opened his eyes, the light faded away. As he turned, he saw his wife who had teased him—and who did not believe—on her knees, crying and praying, for now she believed. She overheard him praying, and as she came into the room, she saw and heard the voice. Then she knew now that they were totally at peace with each other and truly one with God.

MAN THINKING ABOUT DANIEL WEBSTER

A man was sitting in his favorite chair, reading a book, when he came across a word he had not heard of before. So he picked up the *Webster* dictionary and found the meaning of the word. Then he looked at the dictionary and remembered the stories he had always heard about Daniel Webster and the devil. He knew that the stories were not true. He leaned back, thinking, "What if? What if it were true?" That was how stories began. Then his mind wandered back to that time long ago, at a time when angels would come down to earth and visit men.

It happened to Noah, Abraham, Lot. At a time when God himself would visit men like Moses. But one man stuck out the most. It was Job, so he picked up the Bible and read the story of Job. He was a good and honest man who believed in God with all his heart. Then Satan came into the picture and told God, "Take away all his wealth. Your Job will be cussing and hating you."

So God said, "We shall see." He started out small, but Job still trusted in God. Even Job's friends were amazed that he still believed and trusted in God. As time went on, Job did not give in, so God took his most precious possession: he took his family, and Job was left alone. So Job, being a righteous man, still prayed and honored God, so Satan lost. And when it was all over, God, in all his mercy, gave back to Job all that he had lost. Can man do that today? He thought, maybe yes, maybe no. For man today has lost touch with God. Remember, they turned away from his son. But God knew they would. That's why he sent his son, Jesus, to earth for one purpose, and one purpose only: to die on the cross for our sins. Miracles do happen. They happen all the time whether we believe in them or not. You have heard people say, "It's a miracle they survived." Miracles happen every day. You went to work and returned home without getting hit by another car. In today's world, we could say that that was a miracle.

He smiled as he closed the book and the story of Job.

For Mr. Webster wrote a good book. Like the Bible, it is read every day. The dictionary is used for finding out the descriptions to words.

The Bible is read for nourishment of the soul.

He closed his eyes and smiled and thought, "I prefer the Bible, for it's the only book that gives comfort to my soul."

THE GOOD SAMARITAN

A man fell down on the sidewalk as he was leaving a bar all because he had too much to drink.

People walking by were looking down at him and shaking their heads in disgust and kept on going and not looking back. This went on for a while. The man tried to get up, but his legs were too wobbly and weak. It was an embarrassment to himself and also to others who had seen him in that condition. Why then, if it was an embarrassment to others, why didn't they stop and help?

Yes, we know. They, or we, don't want to get involved. That's the trouble with us. It's "mind your own business, don't get involved; he got himself in this mess, so let him get his self out. It's not my concern." Makes you stop and think, doesn't it? We've all said it at one time or another. What if the situation was reversed, would you want someone to stop and help? Yes, you would. Don't lie about it. At one time or another, most of us have fallen on hard times. The Good Book says, "Do unto others, and you would have others do unto you."

A lot of us give to those in need. When you give, no matter how large or small, it makes you feel better from deep down inside. Remember the Good Samaritan. Others passed the man and would not help, but the Good Samaritan helped him, fed him, and even gave him a few coins to help him on his way. So do what you can to help. It may be someone next door. And when you do, you will feel better about yourself. And when that time comes, you will be rewarded.

For you never know. For that one you're helping, you don't even know his name. He may be testing you, and your reward may be just a smile or a handshake. So maybe that reward may be here or that other place, but you will never know unless you try. Try it from your heart, and that feeling, that wonderful feeling that comes from deep down inside when that happens, then you will know, for someone will also notice you and look down on you with a smile.

THE DREAM

I dreamed that I was walking down the street when I noticed a man, an old man, sitting on the curb, worn and tired. He had no shoes or socks on his feet. Everybody was looking at him and turned and walked the other way. Was this man a leopard? No, he just fell on hard times somewhere along the way. As I watched him and the people going by, this was my dream. I could have changed it if I tried. And then something from deep inside said, "Let the dream run its course. Do not interfere, and later I will tell you why."

The old man never said a word, did not ask for a handout. He just stared off into space. The more I looked, yes, the more I wanted to cry. I watched this scene from early morn to the setting of the sun. No one stopped to help; they just passed him by. Then something happened that I could not believe. A young man no more than twenty or so came to the man and sat next to him and held his hand and began to pray. The young man then offered the old man a place to clean up and shave and said, "I just got my first paycheck, and I would like to share it with you today. For I have been on the streets myself. I just got a job, and I have enough to buy you a pair of shoes and socks. Would you let me do this for you today?"

Then the old man, who had never said a word, smiled and said to the young man, "Peace be with you today and beyond, for you are richer by far than all those who passed me today and did not stop to lend me a hand."

The young man smiled and helped the old man to his feet. As he started to leave and take the old man to his place, the old man bent down and kissed him on his cheek. The young man looked and saw something in those eyes. Then the old man smiled and changed before his very own eyes. He saw someone dressed in the whitest of white, and the warmth he gave went in the young man deep, deep down inside. The young man smiled and went to his knees and began to cry. As the man in white began to fade, he looked at the young man and said, "If all did what you did to each other, you would not be in such a mess. For you would love one another."

The young man said, "I understand, and I will spread the word."

Then the young man and my dream began to fade away. As my dream faded and I was not yet awake, I heard that voice that you don't hear but comes to you from deep inside. It said, "Now do you understand? If not, then I will tell you why. You never know who you will meet, for I send my spirit in many forms. Today I was in your dream. So when you awake, remember what you just dreamed, and carry it with you. For you never know when one day this may happen to you, and then you stop and think and remember your dream. Then do your deed, for you may be helping someone in true need, or you may be helping me. Either way, you, by helping them, you have helped me. And that love you have shown is the love that should be shared by all. I will not forget, for it's the love I shared to you first, that love I shared to you from the cross."

OLD MAN AND THE TOWN

There was a man, he lived by the seashore. And every day, he went out to fish. He did this for sixty years or more. He would get into his boat, row out beyond the waves, catch his catch, and return same as all the years before. Some days, the fish would fill his boat, other days not. Either way, he would keep his share, just what he would need. All the rest, no matter how big the catch, he would give the fish to anyone who asked and asked for nothing in return.

This went on six days a week, but on the seventh, he would take his catch from the day before to church and feed it to the people, and it would be a feast. The man did this all his life. His wife had died, and his kids had all moved away. No one was left for him to tend, so he gave his catch to those in need and the people of the town. Some took advantage of him. He knew what was going on, but still he did not complain. Then one morning, he went out in his boat and never returned. The townsfolk waited until the setting of the sun. Still he did not return, not even his boat. They set out the next day, searching high and low, but they found nothing, not even one splinter from the boat. This went on for six days, and at last the seventh was near, so they stopped searching.

The next day at church, the service was read. For some reason, the church was packed except for one chair. It was vacant, for that was where the old man sat. As they prayed, they asked themselves, "Who will replace the old man, and who will feed the town?"

Then the doors swung open, and a small boy came running up the aisle. "I found his boat, it's just outside."

And the people rushed outside to see if this was true. Lo and behold, the boat was at the bottom of the steps and in one piece. And to their amazing eyes, it was overfilled with fish, all fresh and some still alive, not rotting even though the boat had been missing for a week. As some gathered the fish to prepare for the feast, others went looking for the man, hoping to find him alive and sitting on the beach. As they were about to partake of the feast. Their minds and hearts went back to a certain time and place. The place was the Sermon on the Mount where Jesus fed the multitude with just a few loaves of bread and few fish. And then their hearts were saddened for they knew what they had done. They took advantage of the old man, every day, even Sunday from sunup to sundown. Now they were truly praying for his safe return.

As the weeks, the months, and the years went by, the townsfolk started to forget about the old man and his boat full of fish. They had to start fishing for themselves. Those that fished and brought the catch back kept it or sold it. They didn't give any away. And the young boy that ran up the aisle grew up to be a man. For as a boy, he saw but never said a word. He sailed the boat full of fish that came in from the sea and landed at the church. He saw the old man getting out of the boat and smiled at him, waved, and said good-bye. The boy, now a man, stood before the congregation and looked down at the empty chair. He opened the book and read the Sermon on the Mount, and as he read, a beam of light shone through the glass and settled on the empty chair. This boy, now a man, looked at the chair and saw the light. Then with tears in his eyes, he told them all. When he had finished, the people had tears streaming down their face, and they prayed for forgiveness to the old man and, above all, to God. As the man closed the book, he said, "The Sermon on the Mount, that sermon tells it all. Look out for each other, help those that are in need. And when you're out there fishing, think of the old man, and remember what he had done. And maybe if the good Lord is willing, another miracle will occur to one of you. Yes, we can pray it will occur to all of us. Yes, even the whole town."

THE DRUNK AND HIS BOTTLE

A man sitting at a bar with a drink in his hand was arguing to others that there was no God. Most did not argue at all. They just got up or turned the other way. So he finished his drink, got up, and left. He was driving home from the bar, traveling at a high rate of speed, weaving back and forth. Then he ran a red light, and everything went black. When he opened his eyes, he was looking down at himself. As he looked around, he asked, "Why am I up here, yet I'm also down there with people in uniform standing all around?"

Then his mind went back to that hour at the bar when he was arguing to others about their belief in God. As they looked at him, they started to fade away. Then he saw himself as a young boy, then a teen, then a young man. And at the same time, his life was before him, and it showed him all the things that he did. Some were good; some were bad. Then he went back again to when he was a teen. And he saw his father get shot and died there at the scene. He asked, "Why? Why him? He was a good man, a father of five, a good husband. Why him? Why not someone else?"

As time went by, his heart, it hardened. And so did his belief in God. No one found his father's killer; no evidence was left at the scene. So the years went by, and now he was a man drifting from job to job. The bottle was his only friend. The other members of the family went on with their lives. He missed his father so much that at times he just wanted to die. As he looked down at his body and the medics working on him, he also saw lying on the ground a man, a woman, and a child no older than ten.

He heard the medics say, "I don't think anyone will survive." As he looked at himself and especially the child, he cried out. And before you knew it, he was calling out to God, "I'm a drunk, an alcoholic. I deserve this, but don't let them die. Take me instead. No one will miss me when I'm dead."

Then a light brighter than the sun came to him then stopped and said, "I am God's beloved son. You have seen your life go before you. Now you will see what it could have been."

And he saw. Then someone stood before him, someone from long ago. It was his father, all dressed in white, smiling at him like he did that terrible night. That night when his heart went cold and he could not forgive. Then he saw someone he had never seen before. He said, "I'm the one who killed your father. I asked God through his son to forgive me for what I had done. Then I died. Now I'm here. Will you forgive me? Your father did, so did God and his Son."

As the man looked at them both, then down at the bodies on the ground, the man told his father's killer, "I will forgive you." Then he looked at the light and said, "Please, don't let the family die."

The light, it became brighter. The voice said, "You don't care for yourself. You're asking help for the three." And then, before he could blink his eyes, the man opened his and asked the medics if the others were alive.

Now a few years later, the man had been preaching the Word of God. Some say it was a miracle that they all had survived. And the family that was in the wreck, they were sitting in the front pew. For they all shared the same story of that night when they almost met the man in black, the man called the angel of death. Now they knew that when that time came, the one from the light will take them to the other side.

MAN AND DEATH

A man lay dying in bed, with a disease that could not be cured. He looked around and saw four bare walls that seemed to close in on him. He thought to himself, "How long will it be before death pays me a visit and then takes me away?"

He was alone with just the staff to take care of him, so he closed his eyes and tried to get some sleep, wondering if death would come and take him before he awakened. As he closed his eyes, tears rolled down his cheek. He thought about his family and all the good times he had missed. It was his fault his family had left him. He put his work, his job, before all else. They tried not once, not twice, but many times to get him to slow down and put his family first. But things didn't go as he planned. He worked harder to support those that he loved, until one day he returned home to find a note, which he read. His wife was right. His work meant more to him than his family did.

Now it had been many a year. He supportes his family still. His work left him rich, yet something left him empty deep down inside. Twenty years have passed; his kids were now grown. He wondered, when he's gone, would his children come to pay their respects, or will he be buried all alone?

As tears filled his eyes and rolled down his cheeks, something clicked. Not once in his adult life has he prayed. Why? For he did not believe in God. For he believed that once you were dead, you were dead. And the angel or Mr. Death, they were just a myth. But yet something deep down said different. So he tried to put it aside. Then a voice came to him and called his name. As he opened his eyes, a light brighter than the sun was in front of him. The voice said, "I am he that is alive but was dead. I am your salvation, and yet you don't believe. I have been with you from the time you were born. Now death approaches, and you still don't believe. God the Father gave you that inner being that is called your soul. I am here to show you the things that you fear the most. Then it's up to you to choose."

Then the light showed him the place he feared most. That place was so bad that he could not even describe a place of torment that went on and on. Then he remembered his work, his job. It went on and on. As he cried, he asked for help. Then something happened deep down inside. He felt the pain from his sickness go away. He heard the voice say, "Now you're my son, and I will never go away. There will be no angel of death when that time comes, only me. I then will carry you away and take you to my home." He opened his eyes, and he were no longer in pain. He looked and saw his family by his side.

Now he knew there was a God. Now he truly believed. His family told him of a light that each had seen, and the light told them to come. The light said, "You needed each other."

Now weeks have passed. The family was healed, a miracle. His disease went into remission. Now he thanked God for the precious time he's had with his family. Now he thought to himself, "Your Mr. Death will pass me by, for when that time comes, he will come hold my hand as he carries me away into the light to the other side."

ALIENS

As the sun rises in the east and sets in the west, that's when the moon and the stars come out and shine at their very best. As I lay on my back on a clear summer night, out in the country away from the city lights, as I gazed up at the wonders of the Milky Way with all those billions of stars staring down at me, I wondered, yes, I wondered, is there any life out there beyond the stars in our own Milky Way? And if there are, and I assume there might be, what do they look like? Do they look like you or me or some other life-form like you see on TV?

Are they visiting us now as they might have in the past? And if so, why don't they communicate with us? Or are we too barbarian for them to come down and say hello? They slip in and out past our radar, so do they watch us up close or from afar? Maybe some are living with us right in our own backyard, for we don't know what they look like, and we just hear stories that happened to some who said they were abducted by those aliens. Lots of people see ships of different sizes and shapes just floating in the air then taking off, as we say, at the speed of light, traveling so fast we know they're not ours.

Or are we using their technologies from their ships that crashed here on earth? And do we have their bodies frozen in places? Such as Wright-Pat, do we have an organization in our government so secret that even the president doesn't know? You mention Area 51 or Roswell or other events that you have seen. That's when you were told by the men in black you had better not talk, so be quiet. Since that time at Roswell, sightings have been seen from one to a whole city, with thousands looking on. From Mexico City to the Belgium countryside, from police officers to air force pilots to people of renown, they were all not crazy nor were they insane. They were just people going about their daily lives. Then they got taken high up in the sky. Some say they got poked and jabbed and experimented on like rats in a lab. Others say they got impregnated in ways we don't understand. Then in a little while, they were taken again. They take the unborn before it's time. Some say they saw their child after they were taken again.

So why are they abducting us? To them, are we like some, say, rats in a lab? Or are we like blood type O? Is their race dying and they need us to combine with them to create hybrids to keep their race alive? If so, why not just ask? Some will say yes. Some will say no. What would I do if it happened to me? I might say, "Welcome to earth, if you come in peace." But then I just don't know. There must be some truth to all the things we have heard and seen. Thousands of people from all walks of life have seen things that cannot be explained. So as I lay on my back and look up, I think about these ships that have been described by many and have been seen on earth for many, many years.

Even in the Bible, one may be described as Ezekiel's Wheel. Whether we believe or not, this phenomenon will not go away. Most people today believe; some believe in a different way. So as I look up and see all those stars in the universe on a clear night, is there one or a few others that will support life? God created the universe with billions of galaxies and trillions of stars and planets in each. Why only us? We don't need those galaxies, just our own to give us light so we can see. For those other galaxies, we can't see them. They're billions of light-years away. Or did God put them there for a purpose? For aliens or even people that might look like you or me. If he wants us to know and understand and we can love each other and shake and hold each other's hands.

Then maybe he will let them come down, land, and be seen. Then we can join together with them in peace. It may be better for you and me. Only God knows, and only time will tell.

THE LITTLE GIRL

A man was sitting at the table with a cup of coffee, his wife by his side. They were looking at an empty chair across from them, with tears in their eyes. The chair had been empty now for many a year. They were both in their late thirties. Still it was hard to accept that their little girl ten years before lost a battle with life. She was only ten when death took her away. They did everything they could. Their little girl fought very hard and was not afraid. Then, on her last day, she told her parents, "Don't be sad or mad, for things like this happen. For it's a part of life."

Then she told them of the man she met. He told her, "When death comes and it's not far away, I will be with you every step of the way. On the other side there's a place so beautiful it's beyond belief. It's my home. I will take you there in a second or a blink of an eye. One moment you're here, the next you're on the other side."

She told them who he was and for them not to worry, for she would be in his care. She said, "Then one day, many years down the road, when death pays each of them a visit, remember me and what I told you about the man. Believe in him. He will take you to the other side."

So on this day, ten years to be precise, they both wondered, "Did she see the man at the time of her death? And did he take her to the other side?" After they had coffee, they went to their little girl's grave. Each said a silent prayer, praying that she was right and that the man she saw had kept his word and she was with him and she was all right. After ten years, their hearts were still in pain. It was cold and heavy with rain, same as on that sad day ten years past.

After they prayed, they started to leave. Something happened, and they could not believe their eyes. The clouds came apart like the opening of the blinds. The sun showed through just enough to bathe them in a warm glow. The sun settled directly on her grave. They fell to their knees and began to pray. Then a miracle happened. To most people, if you told them this, they would not believe. A yellow rose appeared and came to bloom. The miracle was there was no bush to bare the bud, for it was her favorite out of all the flowers she loved. Then they knew where she was, and she was all right.

The man kept his promise. To them, that was all right. They kept this to themselves and told no one, for who would believe? The rose at the grave, it disappeared in the same manner as it appeared in a blink of an eye. So now they, both, yes, they believe. A few years have passed. The empty chair is not empty anymore, for the parents, they will still miss and love their little girl. But for now, they must go on. For in that chair sits their second child, a boy. Now because of the rose and what their little girl had said. He will forgive and take you to the other side when that day comes, in a blink of an eye.

LUCKY SEVEN

I live in an older and nicer neighborhood. Most of the houses are from around 1890 up to the 1920s. The area had went downhill over the years until around 1980 when younger people, both married and single, bought homes. Some had up to ten rooms at a very nice price. A lot of the older folks sold and moved into smaller ranch condos or regular condos. There was no mowing the lawn and all the upkeeps of maintaining older homes. I was one of the lucky ones. I bought my home in 1985. The price of the house was priced right. Guess for one thing, it was one of a very few houses that was never changed since it was built in 1895, a mixture of Queen Anne, Gothic, and a touch of early Victorian. Large rooms and the attic was a ballroom in itself, all wide open.

Over the years, they put up wood panels on all sides of the attic with a door on each side so they could store things and have the total center part as another room. There were twelve rooms in this house. Why did I ever buy it? Guess it was cheaper than the smaller houses. I found out later why I got it so cheap. The heat bill was more than my house payments. Lucky I could do a lot of the repairs myself. The biggest problem was the furnace. It was a coal furnace converted to gas. That was the first thing that had to go. So at that time, we could change the house on the outside any way we wanted. It was my house, so no one could tell us what color we could not use. To me, if it's your home, fix it up nice. You're the one that is paying for it, not some committee. And some of those that sit on the board don't even know what a Queen Anne or Gothic looks like.

So after I bought it, the first thing I had done was put in spray foam from top to bottom. The windows were next. They were very bad, so I had a company make the same style but with triple panes. At that time, most were double. Then after checking everything out, I arranged to have central air and a new furnace put in. As big as the house was, I had two of each put in. In the long run, it was cheaper, and I had some ducts that would pull the air from the top floors back down to the first. That saved even more. Heat rises, so a fan pulled the heat from the ceiling down the wall to the floor of the first floor. That cost something to do, but over the years, it did pay for itself.

The inside was nice. All original, with a fireplace in every room. Even they were converted to gas that put out heat. In the winter, the upstairs was blocked off. I converted a back room off the study and used it as a bedroom in the winter. So over the years, ten to be precise, the house was complete inside and out. But there's that saying "when it's finished, something else pops up." Repairs were always around the corner so to speak.

During that time, I had two loves in my life: Andy, my mixed-breed, a collie and husky mix. And Jack, a baby stray cat I found in the street about three months old and half dead. They became the kids I never had. I was lucky I stayed at home and worked. I did commercials for large companies and new products. I would go to the company, look at the product, or they would send the product to me, whether it was food, toys, or what. Then I would write at least six tunes or whatever it was and send it back. They would pick out the ones they wanted, or sometimes they would take all. Plus I wrote short stories for monthly magazines. That's how I made my living.

On the street where I lived, most of the homes were the oldest but not the largest. We would all have a once-a-month cookout. Winter, a cook-in; everybody took turns. That way, we got to know everyone. Our street, you could say, was an international street. Also a few were of different religions, but we all shared the same vision. Live in peace with each other and get to know them and their customs. And yes, a little about their religion in case something came up. At least you would know something to say in response to a question. Then as life went on, after thirteen years, Andy passed away while he was asleep on my bed. His ashes were on the mantel in the front parlor.

It was hard for me, even for the neighbors. They loved Andy. He met them all at the front door. And with Jack always by his side, it was harder for Jack. They slept together. When he died, I left him there and brought Jack in so he could see Andy. And then in his way, he will know Andy was no longer with us. So Jack stayed with Andy all afternoon. Then someone came by, and after I said good-bye Andy was taken. The next afternoon, I received Andy's ashes. Every night for a month and sometimes during the day, Jack would sleep where Andy had died.

Then in three years, Jack got sick and he passed away. So now they were both on the mantel. Now it has been five years. There was no one on my bed but the memories. Never again, I vowed, never again would I have pets only to watch them grow old and die. But then that's life. The neighbors offered to get me one, but I said no. So here I sat in a twelve-room house, writing stories, not having to stop in between to give some fur balls a rub on their tummy or a pat on their head. It was an empty house. Guess I was meant to be a loner. Tried affairs, but one way or another, they hated cats or dogs or said that this house was old. I'm into new or retro. Sorry, guess I'm old-fashioned. I love quality and antiques. My house looks like you have just stepped back in time a hundred or more years. I love it. And today, people want retro or modern, so I can buy what I like at a very special price, just like when I purchased this house back in 1985.

One large house two streets over, they bought it only a few years back. Outside it had to remain original; inside they gutted it. It looked like a brand-new modern condo with all new chrome and glass furniture. They invited me in because my house was larger but similar. They removed all the woodwork. Everything. I never asked them why they moved in this area. For the price they paid for the house, they could have bought four condos and connected them all into one for less the price. But it was not my house, but they seemed like very nice people. The people in my area all know each other. We watch out for each and everyone. You would have to drive to the store or other stores. They moved out years ago. But now about three blocks away is a carryout, been there for over fifty years, just sold a small amount of beer. It was a deli, and people would go there instead of driving to the store for a single item.

On a Saturday, I slept in, and when I got up, it was around eleven. And for the first time, there was no coffee in the house, so I slipped on some pants and walked down to the carryout and bought a can of coffee. I talked to a few people and headed back home. But instead of the main street, I cut through the alley. Our alleys were kept clean. A couple of houses were up for sale, and one house was in very bad shape. Even the garage was ready to fall down. It had been boarded up for five years. The family was in court over the estate. So the court ordered the sale. As I neared the garage, I was saying to myself, "Boy, this would make a great house once the garage is torn down. That's when I heard a sound, crying or moaning coming from inside the garage. All I could think of was that someone left a baby. It happened not long ago.

A baby was found in a Dumpster near a hospital. As I neared the door, it was ready to fall down. The sound was coming from inside.

Instead of going home and calling the police, I forgot to take my cell with me. I eased the door open. The sound was at the other end. It was dark inside, so I opened the door, and the light filled the garage. As I walked past all kinds of junk, there in the corner was what was making the noise. Some kittens all crying together with their eyes just starting to open, waiting for their momma to return and nurse them. As I looked at them, I didn't believe this: one, two, there were more as I counted. In total, there were seven little balls of fur. Boy, your momma must have set a record. As I looked, they were all alive.

I said, "Momma will be back soon to feed you." As I turned about four feet away, I saw their mother. It must have been hard having seven and trying to raise them to adults. She must have died during the night.

I said, "Well, sorry little ones, for your loss. Now what am I to do?" As I looked around, there was only one thing to do. So I picked them all up using an old dirty towel and carried them and the coffee can home with me. I placed them in an empty box and went back for the mother, closed the door, and buried her in the backyard near a rose bush. This was better than putting her in a garbage can. She died trying to raise so many.

I went back in, got a large plastic bin, got my heating pad and a couple of soft towels, turned the pad on very low, placed it in the bottom of the storage bin, and put the towels over it and put the bin in the dining area. Then I waited for a few minutes to make sure the pad was not too hot. I then picked up the box, and one by one, I checked them out: five girls, two boys. After I placed them in the container, I started to take them to Pet Rehab. They didn't put any down. Then something inside just told me to raise them. I said to myself, "I can do that, I'm here all the time. Then when they are old enough, I'll find them good homes. None for me, I've lost two that I loved very much, that's enough."

So I got into the car, went to a pet store, got seven bottles and other items for the kittens, and became a mother to seven babies so small I could put two in my shirt pocket. When I returned, I parked in front instead of the back. As I got out, the neighbor across the street was pulling some weeds out of the side yard. She said, "Hi, what's up?"

All I could say was, "I've got seven babies I'm babysitting."

With a strange look on her face, she came over. "Did I just hear you say you were babysitting seven babies?"

"Yes, Peg. Would you like to see them?"

"I sure would. Let me pull off my shoes, they got mud on them."

As they entered, there in the dining area were the kittens.

"Aaron."

"Oh, I'm sorry, Peg. I just said it the wrong way. Here they are."

"You got to be kidding. Seven kittens."

"I just found them an hour or so ago, heard them crying in the old garage down the alleyway. Found the mother. She was dead, so I buried her in the backyard. She raised them this far, guess it was too much for her. So I did what was right, no garbage can for her."

"Aaron, what are you going to do with seven little ones?"

"Well, I'll raise them till I can put them in a fine home. Do you want one or two?"

"None, thank you. But I would love to have them all. But I've got three. Are you going to keep any?"

"No, no, not after Andy and Jack. None for me. I'll be their adopted father for a while. Now if you don't mind, you can help me feed them, I have bottles."

"What's this cord?"

"Oh, electric pad, it will keep them warm."

So within the half hour, they got their first taste of milk off Aaron's finger, and they went for the nipple, and the rest all followed.

"They said one bottle every four hours. And no more, they may get the runs if I give any more. And when they do their thing, I'll just change their bed when I have to. I'll find them a good home."

After that, Peg turned to leave and said, "If you need anything, let me know." As she crossed the street, she yelled back, "And good luck!"

What she said, I needed it. I could just imagine what their mom went through before she died. She was a true mom all the way to the end. I was glad I brought them home even though I was up every four hours feeding them, making sure they were sleeping on dried towels. So twice a day, I changed the towels and fed them.

Then on the third day, I noticed that they were a little bigger and that their eyes were almost open, and I had to feed them more. Within a week, they were all crawling out of the box. So I placed a bunch of towels on the floor and laid them down with them. By the time I put them all on the floor, they were wobbling all over the place, and soon they were all over Mom, me. All had short hair and all were different but all had a V mark on their neck just like their mom. Guess it stood for victory. It was a miracle that they were alive when I found them. And there was someone guiding my hand and made me go into the alley. If you have ever owned a cat and raised it from a kitten, then you know the trouble they get into just like their human counterparts.

It was a madhouse. I got a larger storage bin and made a litter box. Trouble was, the box was higher than they could get into. So I built up some old towels and made a walkway up the side of the box then put one in at a time. All they wanted to do was play in the sand like a kid. Then finally, one had to go. He was already in the box. After he got out, the rest followed, and that's all it took. Seven kittens using the same box and some at the same time. It was awesome. But the trouble was they were getting old enough now to be given to good homes.

Then one night, I was playing with them on the floor. I fell asleep. When I did wake up, I couldn't move—all seven were on top of me, asleep. If only I had a camera. I lay watching them, and my mind went back to when Andy and Jack were little and lay on top of me, sleeping. Why? Why was I thinking of Andy and Jack? I slept there all night. The next morning, they followed me into the kitchen. My grandma would say we have a new breed; it's called a kitchen sitter, sitting in the kitchen waiting for a handout. Then the day came when I was putting up a sign in the yard that said Free Kittens. As I was heading out the door, one followed me. I picked it up. A black-and-white kitten. He was my favorite. He followed me everywhere while the others played or slept.

So I sat down on the chair and put him on my lap. He went straight to sleep. Then I wondered about the mother of these seven, what happened to her. Was she born outside in the wild, or did some turkey kick her out when she became old enough or when she came in season? Most cats are turned loose after that cute baby look is gone; they just dump them anywhere. All they have to do is take them to a cat welfare place, no questions. They will take them in and give them new homes. Too many cats are on the streets all because they are turned loose to fend for themselves. They have been raised by humans.

So as I thought about the mother, I got up and picked up the kitten and went back inside. I tore up the signs and sat down, looking at seven balls of fur. What was I about to do? I will regret this one day. That was three years ago. So I named them after the seven dwarfs even though five were female. Had them all fixed. I fixed up the basement in a playroom for them.

And yes, I even have the neighbors and their kids over. We all go to the basement, take a seat, and let the show begin. All seven, they know they are the center of attraction, and they love it. And so do the kids. Would I change anything? No. But I know that one day, and hope it's many, many years down the road, I will have more put on the mantel. But nothing can make me say I made a mistake. They give me joy and love. And like kids, they are a pain in the neck once in a while. You point your finger, say no, and then in a few minutes, you go over and pick them up and give them a hug.

So if you are one that is planning on adopting a kitten or puppy, remember that they grow up to be adults. Just like kids, they don't stay little forever. And if you're one of those that doesn't want your pet and are planning on turning it loose outside somewhere to fend for itself, put yourself in its place. Would you want someone to do it to you?

Take your pet to one of many shelters that don't put any pets down but keep them till they are adopted again.

On the other hand, if you have these types of feelings, don't get any pets. It's best for you and that pet.

This is just a story to tell folks cats and dogs make great pets. I know. I have had three dogs and one cat in my adult life. Those have passed on, and I loved all of them. And yes, I had them all at the same time.

Now I have three cats: Jackie who is sixteen, Thomas who is very big and who is end to end about forty-three inches and sixteen pounds and looks and acts like Tom of *Tom and Jerry*. He was half starved when I saw him in my driveway. Someone turned him loose. He was about eighteen months old and had been abused. But after lots of love and care, he's a big pushover. Then Missy, she looks like a baby tiger. I found her in mid-February when it was zero degree outside and there was an ice storm. She was about seven months old.

Now all three get along fine. If I had to do it again, yes, I would. Oh, Jackie is my oldest and yes, my baby. She was from a farm in Kentucky. The size of a five-week-old kitten, she fit in my shirt pocket. Cats and dogs make good companions for the young and the old and all in between. So if you see one outside and it looks starved and hungry, feed it. You just may end up with a true companion for a long, long time. Regrets, you'll have none. Oh yes, it will make you a better person. I have three. Sometimes people will go overboard and get too many. That's what we see on the news. But three is enough for me. So please adopt and don't abuse, for if you do, it just might lead to a higher form of abuse.

Remember, God put them here on this planet the same as he put us. We are caretakers of all living things. He will smile on us with total love. For we will be taking care of his creatures, and just maybe, he put them here on this earth. So in time, they will be companions to us, us the human race.